Differentiating Instruction *in the* Regular Classroom

How to Reach and Teach All Learners

Diane Heacox, Ed.D.

Foreword by Cindy A. Strickland

Updated Anniversary Edition

free spirit
PUBLISHING®

KH

Library of Congress Cataloging-in-Publication Data

Heacox, Diane.

    Differentiating instruction in the regular classroom : how to reach and teach all learners, grades K–12 / Diane Heacox.—Updated anniversary ed.

        p. cm.

    Summary: "In this updated edition of the popular and trusted guide, Diane Heacox provides a practical introduction to differentiation and explains how to differentiate instruction in a wide range of settings to provide variety and challenge in how teachers teach and in how students learn. Individual chapters focus on evaluation in a differentiated classroom and how to manage both behavior and work tasks. The author describes ways to get to know students and recognize that all have strengths and limitations. Templates and forms simplify planning; examples illustrate differentiation in many content areas. The book is refreshed throughout to reflect today's most effective practices in curriculum design and instructional methods. New features include connections to Common Core State Standards, revised information on multiple intelligences, updated bibliography and resources, and a PowerPoint presentation for use in staff training and professional development. The accompanying CD-ROM provides the PowerPoint and all of the reproducible forms from the book along with further examples of curriculum maps, workcards, and matrix plans. Teachers can print out what they need, when they need it, and can customize forms for their own classrooms and students."— Provided by publisher.

    ISBN 9781575424163—ISBN 1-57542-416-9

 1. Individualized instruction. 2. Cognitive styles in children. 3. Mixed ability grouping in education. I. Title.

    LB1031.H39 2012

    371.39'4—dc23

                                        2012024242

eBook ISBN: 978-1-57542-652-5

Cover and interior design by Michelle Lee

10 9 8 7 6 5 4 3 2

Printed in the United States of America

Free Spirit Publishing Inc.
Minneapolis, MN
(612) 338-2068
help4kids@freespirit.com
www.freespirit.com

As a member of the Green Press Initiative, Free Spirit Publishing is committed to the three Rs: Reduce, Reuse, Recycle. Whenever possible, we print our books on recycled paper containing a minimum of 30% post-consumer waste. At Free Spirit it's our goal to nurture not only children, but nature too!

green press INITIATIVE

Printed on recycled paper
including 30%
post-consumer waste

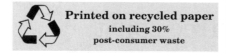

Free Spirit offers competitive pricing.
Contact edsales@freespirit.com for pricing information on multiple quantity purchases.

3/26/14

Dedication

To my husband, John Bloodsworth, for his continual and steadfast love and support, without which I could not "be."

To my daughter, Kylie, for her patience and unconditional love. Your commitment to excellence is a model for your mother.

To all the teachers I have had the privilege to work and learn with worldwide. Your enthusiasm for teaching and your commitment to the success of all students is my continual inspiration.

Acknowledgments

The late Linda King first introduced me to differentiated instruction when I was a novice teacher. Her extraordinary work continues to live with me and those teachers I have the pleasure to serve.

Always thinking about what is good for kids, Judy Galbraith has given me the opportunity to share these ideas with teachers who can make a difference.

My mother, Gloria Heacox, who consistently and persistently supported my personal and professional growth. Proud, positive, loving, and strong, she will continue to be my reference point as I follow my life's journey.

Contents

PART 1

Getting Ready

PART 2

Differentiation in Action

List of Reproducible Pages

List of Figures

Foreword

by Cindy A. Strickland

Recently, I began taking water aerobics at our local pool. As is typical in any group setting, there is a wide variety of participants. Our class includes some who are young, some not-so-young; some already in shape, some hoping to become more so; some who have experience with water aerobics, some who do not; some who love the water, others who are more hesitant. Our instructor, Margaret Ann, sets a welcoming tone as we enter the pool area. She greets everyone with equal enthusiasm, works to quickly learn our names, our backgrounds, and our body "quirks." She makes sure we all have sunscreen and water to drink. Margaret Ann also lets us get to know her—her background, her interests, her own fitness goals. This promotes a feeling of "We're all in this together." Every time this class meets I find myself thinking about ways in which this class models the principles of good teaching in general, and good differentiation in particular.

Margaret Ann's classroom acknowledges and honors differences in learners. She differentiates her lessons almost constantly. Whenever she introduces a new move, she describes three different levels for the exercise. For example, when doing a cross country ski move in the water, she explains that level one is done with shoulders out of the water and a slight bounce on the toes as you "ski." Level two requires that you keep your shoulders underwater and not bounce. Level three is done while not touching the bottom of the pool at all. She tells us to choose the version that is right for us in terms of level of fitness. Here are some examples of what we hear:

"It's *your* choice. Do what feels best to *you.*"

"If you are ready for a more cardio-vascular workout, try level two."

"Level three will work your obliques especially hard."

"If this doesn't work for you, try it this way. The main thing is to keep moving."

"Raise your arms above your head if you want to work on balance as well."

"Use the side of the pool if you need to."

"When you finish your three laps, try adding this move . . ."

"Listen to what your body is telling you."

These kinds of statements provide participants with the information needed to make good choices. Margaret Ann's matter-of-fact tone and body language indicate a total lack of judgment about the decisions any individual may make. As our teacher, her job is to provide excellent modeling, generate excitement and enthusiasm, and provide the individualized feedback we need to improve and to avoid injury. Our job is to identify our own goals and to use her as a resource to help us grow. In this class, we feel empowered and in charge of our own learning. Our teacher shows us that she trusts us and we rise to the occasion.

Granted, my aerobics class is made up of mature adults who have chosen to take the class and are therefore presumably quite motivated. Experienced teachers know that this is not necessarily the case in a typical classroom! The children do not always want to be there. Their level of commitment to doing their best work varies a great deal (sometimes minute by minute!). They may not know how to make good choices when they are offered. Teachers in differentiated classrooms work hard to provide variety and choice, *when appropriate,* and work to teach their students how to make good choices and to value pushing themselves to do things that are just a little bit beyond their current comfort level. All human beings appreciate having a say in what they do and how they do it. If a teacher says to students, "Here is a really onerous assignment for you," they will moan and groan. But if a teacher says, "You have a choice of onerous assignment A or onerous assignment B," students are somehow happier. We must remember that our students live in a world where there is an almost ridiculous level of variety and choice available to them. (A good example is the cereal aisle in the grocery store. Choices include high fiber, low fat, gluten-free, chocolate, strawberry, blueberry, marshmallows, generic, brand name, etc. You name it, they've got it!) When schools focus on a one-size-fits-all, take-it-or-leave-it curriculum, it feels forced and artificial—and maybe even insulting—to our students. No teacher differentiates everything every day. But those of us who are committed to maximizing student learning strive to add to our repertoire of differentiation over time.

Over a decade ago, I took my very first class in differentiation from Diane Heacox. Although that course was a part of a certificate program in teaching gifted students, I remember thinking, "Oh my goodness, all students need and deserve this kind of instruction. I wish I had known about this when I started teaching!" Nevertheless, the first time I consciously tried to differentiate, it took me three hours to plan a 45-minute lesson! If it had continued to take me that long, I probably would have given up and with good reason. But as with any skill set, the more one practices,

the better and faster one gets. I'm at the point now where I can't plan *without* differentiating; it has become such a part of who I am as a teacher.

In this updated anniversary version of *Differentiating Instruction in the Regular Classroom: How to Reach and Teach All Learners,* Diane provides a multitude of practical, teacher-tested tools and templates to help you begin or refine your own journey toward more fully differentiated instruction. She helps us see how current topics in education such as the Common Core State Standards, Response to Intervention, curriculum mapping, and essential questions fit with differentiated instruction. She gives suggestions for gathering information about student needs and preferences. She offers step-by-step approaches to planning lesson content, processes, and products. Throughout this book, Diane's simple, down-to-earth instructions in how to handle the challenges of setting up and running a differentiated classroom helped me, and I am confident they will help you, no matter where you are in your own journey. I wish you well (and don't forget your sunscreen)!

Cindy A. Strickland has been a teacher for 30 years, working with students of all ages from kindergarten to master's degree candidates. In her consulting work, she has provided workshops on differentiation throughout the United States and internationally. Cindy is the author of *Exploring Differentiated Instruction* and the coauthor of *Differentiation in Practice.*

Introduction

The Challenges of Today's Diverse Classrooms

What is your biggest challenge as a teacher? For many, it is attempting to respond to an increasingly broad spectrum of student needs, backgrounds, and learning styles. We know a lot more than our predecessors about why some students learn easily and others struggle. We have useful information about thinking and learning strengths and limitations; about the influence of socioeconomic and family factors on children's school performance and on their access to resources and learning experiences, both within and outside the home; and about the role of gender and cultural background in learning preferences. We know the importance of a student's readiness, learning style, motivation, interests, regard for learning, and confidence. All these factors broaden the range of student needs within a single classroom. But how do we address those needs? And what about the influence of state curriculum standards, graduation requirements, and performance assessments?

Differentiated instruction is a way of thinking about teaching and learning. It is also a collection of strategies that help you better address and manage the variety of learning needs in your classroom. How can you diagnose your students' learning needs accurately and practically? How can you provide learning opportunities that increase the likelihood of student success? The answers to these questions are what differentiating instruction is all about.

Differentiated instruction is not a new trend. It is based on the best practices in education. It puts students at the center of teaching and learning. It lets their learning needs direct your instructional planning.

The Goals of Differentiated Instruction

Differentiated instruction enhances learning for all students by engaging them in activities that better respond to their particular learning needs, strengths, and preferences. The goals of differentiated instruction are:

- To develop challenging and engaging tasks for each learner.

- To develop instructional activities based on essential topics and concepts, significant processes and skills, and multiple ways to display learning.

- To provide flexible approaches to content, instruction, and products.

- To respond to students' readiness, instructional needs, interests, and learning preferences.

- To provide opportunities for students to work in varied instructional formats.

- To meet Common Core State Standards and/or state or provincial content standards for each learner.

- To establish learner-responsive, teacher-facilitated classrooms.

About This Book

This book provides a wide variety of strategies for differentiating instruction. As a professional, you'll easily recognize those that make sense to you and the techniques that reflect your style of teaching. A strategy that's easy for one teacher to use may be burdensome for another. At the same time, the way you differentiate instruction for this year's group of students may differ from what works next year. The intent is to introduce many options for differentiation so you're sure to find techniques that work and that you can make your own.

Please keep in mind that no one expects you to differentiate your entire curriculum in one fell swoop, nor is differentiation required in all areas at all times. Start small with a unit or two, or target a particular subject or curriculum area. Spot the places in your curriculum where you know, based on your experiences, that differentiation is urgently needed for your students' success. Use this book to build a repertoire of strategies for differentiating instruction a little at a time.

I believe it's easier to build new strategies on established foundations. Two theoretical models underlie all of the strategies presented here. Although educational research offers many models and frameworks for teaching and learning, I have chosen to differentiate instruction with the aid of Benjamin Bloom's taxonomy of educational objectives[1] and Howard Gardner's theory of multiple intelligences.[2] Most teachers are well informed about these two models and find them both sensible and highly applicable. Use them as lenses for differentiation, as productive ways to look at what you do in your classroom. Bloom's levels of thinking and learning enable you to recognize and enhance the challenge level in your teaching. Gardner's multiple intelligences provide a ready-to-go technique to increase the variety in how you teach and how you ask your students to learn.

This book will give you a foundation in the principles of differentiated instruction. It will also give you plans, formats, and strategies to make this way of teaching attainable and manageable. You'll find guidance and practical suggestions for addressing the instructional needs of all your learners. It can help you recognize learner diversity and respond instructionally to those differences.

Throughout the book are practical and easy-to-use strategies that you can implement right away; it also offers more comprehensive planning formats for differentiating curriculum units.

You'll find ideas about managing and evaluating differentiated assignments throughout the book. Everything in these pages comes either from my experience as a classroom teacher or from the practical advice of teachers I have worked with as an instructional specialist, professor of education, or professional development trainer.

Chapter 1 describes the diversity of learners in today's classrooms and the implications of these differences for teaching. It presents an overview of differentiating content, process, and product, and an overview of the role of the teacher in a differentiated classroom. It includes questions and answers about differentiation and concludes with an inventory that will enable you to identify the degree to which you currently differentiate instruction.

Chapter 2 engages you in the first step of differentiation: gathering information about your students. It includes ideas on how to solicit information about students from their families. Tools are provided to help you discover your students' interests, learning preferences, readiness, and academic progress.

You'll examine what's important to teach in **Chapter 3**. Working from the Common Core State Standards or the content standards established by your state or province, the chapter guides you through the process of writing essential questions and unit questions to frame and focus your curriculum. You'll find a format for mapping your curriculum and identifying target areas for differentiating instruction. Your curriculum map will serve as a resource in developing other strategies in subsequent chapters.

Chapter 4 identifies challenge and variety as critical elements in differentiating instruction. It suggests using Bloom's taxonomy as an indicator of challenge and Gardner's multiple intelligences as an indicator of variety. The chapter introduces two planning formats for identifying the degree of differentiation within your existing curriculum units. You'll also find a formula for writing more challenging, varied activities.

The heart of differentiated instruction is flexible instructional grouping. **Chapter 5** describes

---

[1] *Taxonomy of Educational Objectives: Book 1 Cognitive Domain*, edited by Benjamin S. Bloom (New York: Addison Wesley, 1984).

[2] *Frames of Mind: The Theory of Multiple Intelligences* by Howard Gardner (New York: Basic Books, 2011).

and explains flexible grouping and distinguishes it from other grouping methods commonly used in classrooms. It suggests when and how to group students for learning and presents management techniques.

Tiered assignments (differentiated learning tasks developed in response to students' needs) are the instructional component of flexible instructional groups. **Chapter 6** explains six ways to tier activities, along with guidelines for organization and management. It also offers criteria for making tiering less visible to students, so they'll see assignments as both interesting and fair in terms of the time and work involved.

In **Chapter 7**, you'll find four strategies for providing student choice within a framework of differentiated activities. Pathways plans allow you to present a choice of tiered, alternative activities to students who "loop out" of skills instruction by demonstrating proficiency. Project menus and challenge centers are strategies for presenting a selection of tiered assignments that students can choose from based on interests and strengths. Spin-offs are projects that extend and enrich the curriculum and may involve students in designing their own learning activities.

How to grade differentiated tasks fairly, calculate and record grades, make grades reflect rigor and challenge, and establish quality criteria: these are the subject of **Chapter 8**. "Totally 10," a project-based learning activity, is presented as a strategy for encouraging students to engage in higher levels of challenge.

Classroom management can seem like an obstacle to differentiated instruction. Suggestions for organization and management are sprinkled throughout the book. **Chapter 9** summarizes these ideas and provides more specifics about managing a differentiated classroom.

Even within today's diverse classrooms, two populations require specific approaches to differentiation: special education students and gifted and talented students. **Chapter 10**, which is devoted to these two groups, offers an overview of their needs as well as differentiation strategies.

The appendixes include additional tools that you might find useful in differentiating instruction in your classroom. Appendix A is a reproducible sample letter you can send to your students' families to explain the goals of differentiated instruction. Appendix B offers in-depth suggestions on adding challenge and variety to classroom discussions. These materials will help you design effective questions, tailor discussions to encourage everyone's best thinking, and engage students in challenging dialogue. Appendix C is the Content Catalysts, Processes, and Products (CCPP) Toolkit, which provides a menu-like alternative method you can use in developing differentiated activities.

I sincerely hope that this book becomes a source of ideas from which you can build a repertoire of strategies for differentiating instruction, and that it energizes you and your classroom, increases the likelihood that your students will be successful learners, and enables you to respond to the diversity in your classroom.

Let's get started!

Diane Heacox

PART 1
Getting Ready

CHAPTER 1

What Is Differentiation?

Differentiating instruction means changing the pace, level, or kind of instruction you provide in response to individual learners' needs, styles, or interests. Differentiated instruction specifically responds to students' progress on the learning continuum—what they already know and what they need to learn. It responds to their best ways of learning and allows them to demonstrate what they've learned in ways that capitalize on their strengths and interests. You can differentiate instruction if your curriculum is district mandated, if it is directed by state standards, and even if learning is measured by statewide basic skills exams or performance assessments.

Differentiated instruction is:

■ **Rigorous.** You provide challenging instruction to motivate students to push themselves. You recognize individual differences and set goals for learning based on a student's particular capabilities. You don't set the bar so low that students need not make their best efforts nor so high that students fail and feel defeated.

■ **Relevant.** It focuses on essential learning, not on "side trips" or "fluff." Differentiating does not mean more of the same to fill time (for example, more problems instead of more *challenging* problems); differentiating does not mean activities that are fun for students but don't focus on significant learning. These are side trips and fluff. Differentiating focuses on essential learning.

■ **Flexible and varied.** Where appropriate, students make choices about how they will learn and how they will show what they've learned. They may be given opportunities to select topics they wish to explore in greater depth. They may also choose whether they will work independently, with a partner, or in a group. With differentiation, teachers employ many different instructional strategies. Instruction is not "one size fits all."

■ **Complex.** You don't surf over the top of concepts. Rather, you challenge students' thinking and actively engage them in content that conveys depth and breadth.

Jolenda Henderson's fourth-grade students have been collecting, organizing, and analyzing data in math. Today, they'll be working with line graphs. Students were introduced to line graphs in third grade, but Jolenda has noticed that some are still struggling. Since she knows she needs to provide more time and instruction for these students, she intends to spend today's class reteaching line graphs. First, she'll ask students to gather data from each other, such as who's right-handed and who's left-handed, what everyone's favorite kind of pizza is, and the number of siblings each has. Then she'll draw graphs on the board to represent the data they've collected.

Larry Kimmer's fourth-grade students are also studying graphs in math. Since he knows that graphs were introduced in third grade, he has pretested his students to find out what they recall about data collection and graphing. In the pretest, three students scored at least 85 percent on all concepts he assessed. Ten students scored at least 85 percent on some, but not all, of the concepts. Eleven students' scores indicated that they need practice in both analyzing and representing data.

Based on these results, Larry plans to provide more instruction on line graphs for the eleven students who need review and practice. Once these students have the skills well in hand, he'll ask them to construct their own graphs to represent data he'll provide. For the thirteen students whose preassessment indicates understanding of some or all of graphing, he's designed a menu of activities. The three students who have "tested out" will move immediately to the menu, choosing from activities that ask them to apply what they know or to design original projects collecting and reporting data. The ten students who have mastered some but not all of the skills will "loop" in and out of instruction. They will be with the instructional group when Larry is teaching a graphing skill they need. When he's teaching a skill they've mastered, they will choose from the menu of activities. He has provided supplies for the menu activities and has posted workcards with directions for projects and quality criteria for evaluating them.

Tony Richards has taught his tenth-grade English class about the elements of Shakespeare's tragedies, such as structure, conflict, and denouement. They have just finished reading *Romeo and Juliet.* Judging from yesterday's discussion and written work, Tony knows that about half his students can easily identify the elements and find them represented in the play. The other students are having varying degrees of difficulty both understanding elements and finding them in the play. Today he plans to spend part of the class reviewing the information about elements. Then he'll divide students into groups to create charts explaining the elements and noting examples of each from the play. His students like to work in groups, and he hopes this exercise will give those who are struggling a chance to learn from those who understand the material.

Marie Fuentes's tenth-grade students have also been studying elements in Shakespeare's tragedies and have read *Romeo and Juliet.* Based on class discussions and independent work, Marie has determined that two-thirds of her students understand and can identify the elements of Shakespearean tragedy. The other third are having difficulty both understanding and identifying these elements. Accordingly, today she'll group her students into three work teams to create posters on what they've learned. Team A consists of students needing more direct instruction on elements. She will work with them first and then explain that their poster is to illustrate each element in a creative, visual way. Members of Teams B and C understand the elements and can find examples in the play. They will apply and

extend their knowledge by analyzing whether these elements are also represented in contemporary plays. Their posters will chart examples of the elements from plays they read in the previous unit. These groups are also to represent their ideas in a creative, visual way.

Each team has an identified leader, a sheet explaining quality criteria for evaluating posters, and a workstation equipped with materials. As students move to their stations, Marie joins Team A. This is her opportunity to review the elements with the group before they begin their poster. Once Team A is under way independently, she will move on to Teams B and C to check their progress and answer questions.

Differentiated Instruction: One Size *Doesn't* Fit All

All four teachers in these examples recognized the learning differences in their classrooms. Jolenda Henderson (fourth grade) and Tony Richards (tenth grade) focused their day's lesson plans on the needs of those students who still struggled with content or skills. Both teachers chose to *reteach* material to *all* students, including those who had demonstrated varying degrees of mastery. For other lessons, they would likely move all students forward in the curriculum—a decision that would address only the needs of those ready for the next learning objective and would leave behind those who need more time or instruction to master the current objective. Though they recognized the contrasting learning needs of their students, Jolenda and Tony weren't sure how to plan and manage instruction that required different students doing different activities during the same class period. Their teaching is not yet differentiated.

On the other hand, the teaching of Larry Kimmer (fourth grade) and Marie Fuentes (tenth grade) exemplifies differentiation. Working from their understanding of students' learning needs, both teachers found ways to provide more instruction for those in need without holding back those who were ready for new challenges. Larry retaught line graphs only to those students whose preassessment showed a need for more practice. For students ready to move on, he provided a menu of activities at various "levels of challenge." Similarly, Marie reviewed the material with students who needed it and assigned them an interesting project to demonstrate their understanding. For students ready to move on, she designed a higher-level project so they could apply and extend their knowledge. Marie asked all students to share what they learned in a visual, creative way, rather than a more typical language-arts product that focused on reading, writing, or speaking. The posters enabled Marie to reach those students whose learning strengths are spatial, rather than verbal.

Differentiated classrooms reflect teachers' thoughtful diagnosis of students' learning needs and purposeful planning of activities and projects that address those needs. In today's diverse classrooms, often one size doesn't fit all.

You May Be Differentiating Already

The first step in differentiating instruction is to start where you are. Good differentiation does *not* require throwing out all your planning from the past two, five, ten, or fifteen years. And many teachers have been using differentiation strategies without even knowing it. Good differentiation means examining how well you're providing variety and challenge in learning, identifying who among your students is best served by your current plans, and modifying those plans as needed so more students can be successful learners.

Differentiation is a two-step process:

1. Analyze the degree of challenge and variety in your current instructional plans.

2. Modify, adapt, or design new approaches to instruction in response to students' needs, interests, and learning preferences.

Our Diverse Classrooms

All students have individual learning preferences, backgrounds, and needs. Today, educational research enables us to better identify those variables that can affect a student's performance in school. Once you're aware of the differences that can exist, you're better able to differentiate your instruction to reach as many students as possible. Here are several examples of learner diversity in today's classrooms.

Cognitive Abilities

In the past, psychologists and teachers narrowly defined cognitive abilities based on students' scores on standardized intelligence tests or aptitude tests. Now, thanks to the work of educational leaders like Howard Gardner, the definition of intelligence, or "being smart," has broadened. Gardner's theory of multiple intelligences suggests, among other things, that students' thinking strengths and limitations affect not only the ease with which they learn, but also how students can best represent what they know. For example, when asked to read, write, or speak, a student with verbal/linguistic strengths will always have an edge over a student with lesser verbal capabilities. On the other hand, the verbal/linguistic student may be at a disadvantage if the measure of learning is a role play or skit that calls on bodily/kinesthetic skills. (For more about Gardner's theory, see Chapter 2, pages 22–25.)

In differentiated instruction, teachers design activities that support students' learning preferences and strengths while presenting tasks that encourage growth in areas of weakness. The more ways you can engage students in learning—giving them more opportunities to use their preferred ways of thinking—the better their ability to learn. When instruction and assessment are modified according to learners' unique needs, the likelihood of success increases for all students, whether regular education students, students with learning difficulties, or those with limited English proficiency. **In some ways, differentiated instruction gives every student the specialized instructional focus that's long been provided for special education students through individualized education plans. But what differentiated instruction**

provides is more manageable, more efficient, and easier for teachers to implement.

Learning Profile

Learning profiles reflect individual preferences for where, when, or how a student obtains and processes information. Students' profiles represent their preferences related to learning modalities, their personal and curricular interests, as well as cognitive preferences. Educators and researchers hold various theories about learning profiles, each of which offers another way of looking at the diversity in our classrooms.

Some learning theories focus on elements such as environment (light, temperature, sound), social organization (working alone, with a partner, or on a team), physical circumstances (degree of mobility, time of day), emotional climate (motivation, degree of structure), and psychological factors (whether a student is reflective, impulsive, or analytic).[1]

Other theories focus on learning modalities: sight, hearing, and touch.[2] *Visual* learners process information most effectively when they can see what they're learning—for example, through reading, writing, and observing. *Auditory* learners need to hear information to help them learn—for example, through oral presentations and explanations. *Kinesthetic* or *tactile* learners learn best when they can manipulate objects or materials—for example, by doing, touching, and moving.

Today, most teachers are familiar with Howard Gardner's multiple intelligences. Gardner's work is focused on cognitive or thinking preferences. Thus far, his model presents eight cognitive preferences: verbal-linguistic, logical-mathematical, visual-spatial, bodily-kinesthetic, musical, interpersonal, intrapersonal, and the naturalist. In addition, he notes the existential as a tentative ninth preference.

Differentiated instruction allows you to reach more learners through thoughtfully examining your students' learning profiles and using this data as a lens to inform your instructional planning.

Socioeconomic and Family Factors

Students' backgrounds and home lives have a profound effect on their school performance. You can't assume that all students have similar home environments or the same opportunities outside of the classroom.

If a child is hungry, tired, or stressed, or if he or she lacks a place to study, the ability to learn is affected. Family members may have limited time for helping with children's education, for example, by assisting with homework. Some students' home life is disrupted by chemical dependency, mental illness, physical disability, divorce, or abuse. In some homes, learning and education aren't emphasized or consistently supported. Some parents' high-pressure careers, frequent travel, or long work hours can create a home environment in which an adult isn't always present to monitor, advise, or direct children and teens. Or a parent may simply feel unprepared to help with school assignments.

Students' access to resources and learning experiences outside of school also varies. Not all kids have basic school supplies; not all kids can get to a library. The "digital divide" has created an information gap between kids with computers at home (specifically, Internet access) and those without. While some students' families discuss issues together and travel (whether exploring their own neighborhoods or beyond), other families may be less involved.

A student who has access to resources and enriching experiences may come to school with a greater foundation for learning and a greater depth of understanding than a student who lacks such advantages. Children with actively engaged and supportive parents receive a strong message about the value of learning, a message that can affect their level of motivation and commitment. Differentiated instruction doesn't assume all students are starting at the same level of learning with the same family support and involvement.

[1] See, for example, two books by Rita Dunn and Kenneth Dunn, *Teaching Elementary Students Through Their Individual Learning Styles: Practical Approaches for Grades 3–6* (Boston, MA: Allyn & Bacon, 1992), and *Teaching Secondary Students Through Their Individual Learning Styles: Practical Approaches for Grades 7–12* (Boston: Allyn & Bacon, 1993).

[2] See, for example, *Applying Educational Psychology in the Classroom*, 5th ed., by Myron H. Dembo (New York: Longman, 1994).

Readiness

As you prepare to introduce new content or skills, you recognize that some students are ready for what you are about to teach, some lack the foundational skills to move on, and some know the material already (or even knew it last year). Some children, particularly those who have had early learning opportunities, begin school with well-developed skills and considerable understanding of various topics; other students arrive as true beginners. **Our challenge as teachers is to find ways to build on and extend the learning of students who are already on their way, while providing basic instruction and practice for students who are beginning or struggling.**

Learning Pace

Students vary in the amount of time it takes them to master a skill or learn a concept. Some will grasp most material right away; for example, many gifted and talented students learn in one-third the time that average learners need. Since they learn rapidly, the gifted and talented students require fewer examples, less modeling, and shorter practice time. Other learners need more instruction, examples, practice time, and feedback to be successful. Differentiation helps teachers develop lesson plans and activities that keep children from being left behind or waiting to move on.

Gender Influences

Brain researcher Michael Gurian provides insights on how gender may influence learning. He notes, for example, that boys take longer to master reading than girls do; they show early mathematical ability and strengths in three-dimensional reasoning; they prefer action and exploration to passive learning; they benefit from regular physical activity and do best with hands-on learning in reading and math.[3]

Educational researcher Karen Rogers has synthesized research on female learning differences. Her research suggests that girls learn best when their classrooms provide variety in teaching methods; tasks with many possible right answers; activities that use manipulatives and a hands-on, process approach to learning; opportunities to ask questions and discuss ideas and concepts; visual ways to present information; examples of real-life applications; and a variety of social arrangements in the classroom, such as a balance between independent and collaborative work and balance between same-gender and mixed-gender groups.[4]

Do many boys also thrive with these instructional methods? Yes. Do all girls require them to be successful learners? No. **Gender is merely another way to look at student diversity. If you know something about girls' and boys' similarities and differences in learning styles and strengths, you can provide a balance in teaching methods so that all students are more likely to succeed.**

Cultural/Ethnic Influences

Another influence on learning, although somewhat controversial, is a student's cultural or ethnic background. Geneva Gay, professor of education at the University of Washington–Seattle, has been an active contributor to our knowledge of culturally and ethnically diverse learners. In her view, children begin school with an internalized learning style, including rules and procedures for acquiring knowledge and demonstrating skills. They have developed these ways of learning partly through their experiences within their cultural or ethnic group.

Although Gay agrees that models such as Gardner's multiple intelligences and Bloom's taxonomy have application for all children, she notes that certain learning preferences may be influenced by a child's group identity and affiliations. (For more information about Bloom's taxonomy, see pages 73–76 in Chapter 4. For more information about Gardner's multiple intelligences, see pages 22–25 in Chapter 2.) It's important not to assume, however, that all members of a group will learn best the same way. There are

[3] *Boys and Girls Learn Differently!* by Michael Gurian (San Francisco: Jossey-Bass, 2010).
[4] *Challenges of Promise* by Karen B. Rogers, a Title II Research Report (Edina, MN: Edina Public Schools, 1990).

great variations in learning preferences within any group. As with the influence of gender on learning, you can differentiate instruction more effectively when you recognize style preferences among students from various cultural and ethnic groups.[5]

How Students Value Learning

Differences in the value students place on learning and education also affect classroom diversity. Teachers know that when students are interested in and value what they're being taught, they engage in activities with greater commitment, enthusiasm, and motivation. Some students care about what we want them to learn and some don't. How much an activity or topic is valued may reflect an individual student's sense of how relevant or usable the material is. It's a fact of school life that not every topic and activity will interest all learners. However, if you make a point to find out your students' interests, you're better able to devise lessons and assignments that will motivate them.

Students are also affected by family attitudes. If parents or other significant adults highly value a particular subject, chances are the student will, too. Likewise, if adults see little importance in a subject, they may give the student "permission" (tacitly or directly) not to care about it. Some families place a strong emphasis on learning and school success. They see a good education as essential for their children's future. Other families don't see education as a means to a successful, satisfying life. Although some students may embrace beliefs and values about school that are contrary to those of their families, most are influenced by their family's beliefs.

Similarly, if a student's friends value learning and school achievement, this will influence the student's attitude toward education. If a student's friends dislike school or have little interest in learning, the student may come to feel the same way in order to fit in.

When you can respond more specifically to students' interests—and when you show the application of learning to life—you're better able to appeal to your more reluctant learners.

Confidence in Learning

Students who say to themselves, *I can do this, I can figure this out, I am good at this,* learn very differently and are usually more successful than students who tell themselves, *I'm not good at this, this is too hard, I don't get it.* Confident students know that even if they don't succeed in learning something the first time, they will learn it eventually. Students who lack confidence tend to give up or give in to failure. Some students have already decided they can't learn. If you're able to respond directly to individual learning needs and preferences, more students will be confident about their ability to learn and thus be more successful.

What Do We Differentiate?

Differentiated instruction typically involves modifications in one or more of the following areas: content, process, and product.

Content

Content is the "what" of teaching—the curricular topics, concepts, or themes presented to students. Curriculum content is usually determined by the school or district and often reflects state or national standards.

Content is differentiated by concentrating on the most relevant and essential concepts, processes, and skills or by increasing the complexity of learning. Some students need more instruction and practice, and some need less. For students with early or quick mastery, you can eliminate content or speed up its presentation.

You differentiate content (a) when you pre-assess students' skills and knowledge,then match learners with appropriate activities according to readiness; (b) when you give students choices about topics to explore in greater depth; and (c) when you provide students with basic and advanced resources that match their current levels of understanding.

For example, let's say your class is studying historical fiction and all students are required to select a novel and describe the characteristics of historical fiction exhibited in their books. Content can be differentiated by providing a selection of

[5] For more on Geneva Gay's work, see *Culturally Responsive Teaching: Theory, Research, & Practice* (New York: Teachers College Press, 2010).

books that reflect a variety of reading levels and by matching students with the appropriate book. You may simply group books on desks or countertops and purposefully direct students to make their selections from a particular collection.

You can also differentiate content by selecting resources related to a curricular topic, including some that are basic and foundational and others that are more sophisticated, technical, advanced, or in-depth. Specific content resources can be purposefully assigned to students based on their existing knowledge of the topic under study.

Process

Process is the "how" of teaching. In differentiated instruction, the way you teach reflects the learning profiles and preferences of your students. You can modify process by adding greater complexity or abstractness to tasks, by engaging students in critical and creative thinking, or by increasing the variety of ways in which you ask them to learn.

For example, your class is working on comparing and contrasting two versions of *Cinderella* from different cultures. Having decided to assign tasks based on learning profile (see page 8), you assign students to groups of visual, auditory, or kinesthetic learners. The visual learners draw pictures of both similar and different elements of the two stories. The auditory learners discuss similarities and differences between the two versions with partners and prepare an oral presentation. The kinesthetic learners create thirty-second scene reenactments that represent similarities and differences between the two versions. At the end of the work time, all groups share their ideas.

Note that while the content is the same, the ways that students are able to learn or *process* the information is different.

Product

Products are the end results of learning. For example, a product may be something tangible, like a report, brochure, or model; it may be verbal, like a dialogue, speech, or debate; or it may involve action, like a skit, mock trial, or dance. Products reflect what students have understood and been able to apply. They show learning in use and may reveal new thinking or ideas.

The work of Bloom and Gardner helps us differentiate products by providing greater challenge, variety, and choice in how students demonstrate or represent what they've learned. Products are differentiated when you plan units that reflect many ways to represent learning and when you provide menus of projects for students to choose from. You may ask students to create products that match their learning strengths (for example, a student with strong musical skills writes a song or rap), or you may ask them to practice working in the areas that are not their strengths (for example, a student with solid verbal/linguistic skills makes a spatial product like a model or collage). Differentiate products by encouraging students to take on challenging work, to run with their ideas, or to come up with unique ways to show what they've learned.

What Is the Teacher's Role?

As a teacher who differentiates instruction, you become both a facilitator and a collaborator.

You Are a Facilitator

As a facilitator of differentiated instruction, you have three key responsibilities: providing and prescribing differentiated learning opportunities, organizing students for learning, and using time flexibly.

1. Providing and prescribing differentiated learning opportunities. You *provide* a range of activities that challenges students and offers variety both in the ways students learn (process) and in the ways they present their learning (products). Providing greater challenge and variety means responding to more students' learning needs and preferences. At times, you offer students an opportunity to choose what they'll do, how they'll do it, and what their final result or product will be.

At other times, you *prescribe* particular activities that have been specifically designed to meet the needs of particular learners or groups of learners. To do this, you must first get to know your students' interests, degree of readiness, and learning preferences. Then you differentiate by matching particular activities with particular students, based on learning needs.

2. Organizing students for learning. As a facilitator of differentiated instruction, you vary the ways you organize and group students. Depending on the assignment, they may work individually, in pairs, in teams, in collaborative/ cooperative groups, in flexible instructional groups, or as a class. You determine the most effective way to organize them for particular tasks, based on your curriculum objectives and their learning needs.

Students may also be grouped according to their learning preferences or interests. For example, you could group several students with bodily/ kinesthetic preferences for a role-playing activity. Or you could offer opportunities for students to choose their own groups based on their interest in particular topics or projects.

When you group students with common learning needs in flexible instructional groups, students with similar degrees of readiness work together on activities you've tailored to match their specific needs. Sometimes you might have one group working on a basic learning activity and another working on an advanced activity. At other times you'll group students who need more time or instruction on a skill and then form a second group for students who have shown mastery of the skill and are ready to apply what they've learned to a more challenging activity. **Determining the most appropriate ways to organize students for learning is a key task for teachers who differentiate instruction.**

3. Using time flexibly. In a differentiated classroom, you use time in different ways with different students. For those who need more explanation, review, or practice, you extend instructional time; for those who have mastered concepts or skills, you replace reteaching or practice time with advanced learning. For students who need less time to master new material, you may also choose to accelerate learning. In the differentiated classroom, time is flexible and its best use meets students' learning needs.

You Are a Collaborator

Differentiating instruction does require time and effort, particularly when you're just beginning, but you needn't go it alone. You can form partnerships with other staff members and share materials, insights, and resources. Here are some ideas:

■ Combine classes for an activity facilitated by one teacher while the other teacher works on planning differentiated activities for use by both teachers.

■ You and another teacher in your grade level or department might each take a curriculum unit to differentiate and then exchange. Or you might form a differentiation team, dividing the tasks and then sharing the results.

■ Share resources for differentiation to make your budget dollars go further.

■ Work with the media specialist in your school. She or he can be your ally in finding relevant books, magazine articles, materials, and websites.

■ Communicate regularly with other specialists in your school, such as those who work with special education students, second language learners, and gifted and talented students. Like you, these teachers must grapple daily with classroom diversity and they have good ideas on how to reach and teach students with special needs. Ask them for information and feedback on the appropriateness of differentiated tasks for students receiving special services who are mainstreamed in your classroom. Bring them in on your planning. Who can better help you design directed activities than the people whose daily work involves modifying instruction?

Another group of collaborators includes your students' families. In Chapter 2, you'll find ways to solicit the help of parents as you learn about your students' interests and learning preferences. Families are your natural allies in helping more students be successful learners. It is worthwhile to explain what you're doing and ask for their help and support.

Qualities of a Supportive Classroom Environment for Differentiation

A supportive classroom environment is vital to your success in differentiating instruction. Such an environment:

■ Promotes acceptance of differences.

■ Affirms that all students have learning strengths.

■ Acknowledges that students learn at different rates and in different ways.

■ Recognizes that for work to be fair, it must sometimes be different.

■ Acknowledges that success means different things to different people.

■ Allows students to work with various people for various purposes.

■ Recognizes that the key to motivation is interest, and that all students have different interests.

■ Promotes personal responsibility for learning.

■ Builds feelings of personal competence and confidence in learning.

■ Values effort and "personal best."

■ Nurtures skills of independence.

■ Supports and celebrates student success in challenging work.

■ Encourages exploration of each student's interests, strengths, and learning preferences.

■ Nurtures the creative spirit in all students.

■ Honors everyone's work.

Questions and Answers About Differentiating Instruction

Most of us recognize the great diversity of learning needs, styles, interests, and motivations among our students, and we know that differentiating learning activities based on individual differences can increase the likelihood of success for all. So why isn't everyone differentiating instruction? Teachers at all levels ask questions like the following.

I don't have strategies for differentiating instruction. How do I do it?

Many teacher preparation programs provide little beyond general strategies for meeting the needs of special education students and gifted and talented students in the regular classroom. Once teachers are hired, school districts may lack time or professional development expertise to provide in-service training in differentiated instruction. Teachers must often get the training they need on their own.

One way to learn about differentiating instruction is to attend workshops or graduate classes. You might form study teams or book clubs with colleagues in your school to read and discuss books such as this one and then help each other apply the ideas in the classroom. **Once you've been introduced to the strategies of differentiation, you'll probably recognize classroom practices you're already using. Each time you provide a student with extra help, more time, or a modified assignment, you're differentiating instruction. All good teachers, whether they realize it or not, differentiate to some degree**.

As you'll see in the following chapters, you will start with your curriculum and then examine your current teaching practices. At that point, you are ready to modify, redesign, or create activities that differentiate based on students' learning needs. All of this is done one step at a time. No one should feel obligated to tackle all curricular areas or all instructional units in a single school year. Differentiation is a *process*—your skills will develop, your confidence will grow, and the time you need for planning will decrease.

I'm comfortable with the way I teach. If it's working, why change it?

It's human nature to stick with what you know and what you feel works for most of your students. Trying out new strategies is hard work, at least at first, and it can make you feel less secure about your teaching. You may wonder whether this new idea will help or hinder students' learning, whether it's worth the time and effort to change what you've done in the past. Yet most of us can see that, despite our best efforts, some students struggle, some are held back, some are bored, and some are frustrated and discouraged. Chances are, we wonder how to help them and how to do a better job with all of our students.

With differentiated instruction, the focus is not on what you teach but on what students learn, not on what you've covered but on whether students have accomplished their learning goals. When you differentiate instruction, you know you're meeting the learning needs of more of your students. You're increasing the likelihood that all students—not just some—will be successful learners.

My curriculum is determined by the district and influenced by state standards. How can I differentiate when I'm required to teach specific content and skills and when I must prepare students for district or state assessments?

In many schools standards drive curriculum—whether adopted by school districts, required by state graduation rules, or set by national curriculum organizations or agencies. But keep in mind that while standards may direct your curriculum and focus your learning goals, they *don't* dictate what you do instructionally to get students "there."

Differentiated instruction is the best response to standards-based education. You simply cannot get all students to meet the standards unless you differentiate. Teachers and schools are increasingly held accountable for students left behind as well as for students ready to advance who must wait until classmates receive more instructional time. Differentiation, in fact, may be the key to your students' success in a standards-based educational system.

You may assume that differentiation takes more class time—time you simply do not have. **Differentiated instruction, however, allows you to use your time more efficiently.** You adjust pace and depth to the needs of learners and the demands of the curriculum. You eliminate the teaching of specific content or skills for students who have already mastered them. You plan more time and instruction for those who need more practice. **Time may actually be saved as students engage in learning that responds to their needs.** When you provide appropriate individual or small-group projects for some, they work independently and you have more time with students who need your attention. No one is held back or left behind.

The strategies of differentiated instruction can be used to modify and adjust any curriculum to respond to students' needs. **Regardless of how much or how little freedom you have to decide *what* you will teach, differentiated instruction will assist you in deciding *how* you will teach.**

With an already full school day, how can I find the planning time to differentiate instruction?

It's easy to feel overwhelmed with all the changes occurring in schools today. Additional course requirements, increased professional responsibilities, changes in state graduation requirements, statewide testing, and your schools' own reform initiatives are creating greater demands on teachers' time and energy. Paperwork, conferences, faculty meetings, committee meetings, coaching, advising, returning phone calls and email: sometimes it seems like you have less and less time for teaching—and who has time to *prepare* for teaching? Although many of us would like to provide more differentiation, we find little school time for such in-depth planning, and most schools lack sufficient funding for summer curriculum projects.

The answer is to **start small, differentiating one subject or targeting specific units for revision. Remember that you're starting with what you have and then modifying your instructional plan—you are *not* throwing out your units and starting over.** Look carefully at the activities in your text or curriculum guide, decide whose needs are best addressed with each activity, and then design additional activities for reteaching or extending learning as necessary. Think about how you could increase variety in the kinds of activities, projects, and assessments you offer, and thus reach more students.

As suggested in the previous section (What Is the Teacher's Role? pages 11–13), consider trading ideas or activities with a colleague. If each of you differentiates a unit and you trade with each other, you'll have two units ready to go, rather than one. If your colleague is in another school across the district, how about collaborating and sharing via email?

Although differentiating instruction does take time, **one of the rewards is the possibility of using something next year that worked this year. Think of differentiated instruction as cumulative—one unit, one subject, at a time.** Once you have the strategies presented in this book firmly in mind, you can accomplish much more in far less time.

How do I explain differentiated instruction to parents?

In the mid-1990s, when publishers and teachers responded to recommendations by the National Council of Teachers of Mathematics, the math curriculum changed from a focus on computation to a focus on problem solving. Some parents were concerned that students wouldn't learn basic skills, and they felt uneasy because math didn't "look" like it did when they were in school. Many districts needed to orient parents toward the new approaches in mathematics instruction.

In the same way, you may need to explain the goals and methods of differentiation to help parents understand the changes in your classroom. Consider doing a presentation at an open house or during curriculum night. Write a letter to parents at the beginning of the school year or prepare a brochure describing your goals and plans. (For a sample letter, see Appendix A, page 150.)

Some parents are concerned about the effects of different students doing different kinds of activities. Does participation in particular activities give some kids an edge over others? Will some activities appear to be "dumbed down"? Will differentiated instruction make some students seem "better" than others? Parents need to know that teachers differentiate instruction in the best interests of all learners. Differentiated tasks do not mean that some students get the exciting work while others get the dreary drills. Reassure parents that groupings and tasks are always changing, since you are continually monitoring and assessing students' skills and interests. Activities and lessons are planned so that every student has the opportunity to expand his or her knowledge from an individual starting point, and every student has the opportunity to work with students with similar interests, with differing interests, with similar skills, and alone. The purpose of differentiated instruction is to increase the likelihood that all students will be successful—all students, in different ways, at varying paces.

The issue of fairness comes up for parents (and for teachers, too) when students are engaged in different kinds of activities. Some may suspect that not giving everyone the same instruction or assignments is unfair. Concerns about fairness may be particularly strong both for parents of struggling students and for parents of above-average or gifted students. But consider the following:

- Is it fair that students who need more time, practice, or instruction fall further and further behind as the class moves on?

- Is it fair that students who have mastered material must sit through review or wait to move on while other students catch up?

What *is* fair is differentiated instruction—providing what individual students need.

How do I make differentiation "invisible" to students so they don't feel that being assigned different tasks is unfair?

Teachers often wonder how to avoid creating "low" groups and "high" groups when they differentiate instruction—they don't want to fall into the old "bluebirds and buzzards" method of grouping. How can differentiation occur in a low-key way so that students who are placed in groups receiving extra teaching and practice don't feel bad about the situation (and so students doing advanced work don't feel they're getting more work than others)?

Recall the classroom examples of Larry and Marie (pages 5–6). Assuming they differentiate their instruction on a regular basis, their students would know from past experience that the groups they're in one day won't necessarily be the groups they'll be in the next day. The groups these teachers formed were based on students' similar instructional needs. It's when teachers *don't* regularly vary the composition and purposes of groups that grouping draws students' attention. If you're always "mixing things up," students won't focus on the particular people they're working with on a given day.

When you group students for differentiated instruction, do so as an instructional strategy, for various purposes. Sometimes group students of varying abilities and degrees of readiness for collaborative work. At other times, group students with similar instructional needs or let students pick their own groups based on interest in a particular topic or project. Keep in mind that assigning students to groups doesn't necessarily mean they'll be doing a group project or collaborative work—only that all students in that group are assigned the same task. They might work with a partner or independently.

The kind of work students engage in also affects their perception of differentiated instruction. Assigning low-level, paper-and-pencil seatwork to students reviewing or working on basic tasks while more advanced students get exciting,

hands-on projects (the "fun stuff") is a recipe for resentment. Another way to create unhappy students is to assign *more* work, rather than more *challenging* work, to advanced learners. It's crucial that all students find their work relevant, valuable, engaging, and interesting. When you plan stimulating learning activities for everyone, you make differentiated instruction as invisible as possible—it's simply the way students learn in your classroom. Specific ideas will be provided later in this book.

How do I manage my classroom when students are doing different things at the same time?

Challenges arise when you begin to differentiate by grouping students for instruction and providing multiple learning tasks. It can be daunting to figure out whom to group, when to group, what directions to give, and how to monitor students as they work. If you teach in middle or high school, the sheer number of students you see in a day may make you think that differentiating instruction is impossible. It is, admittedly, easier just to keep students together, doing the same activity. It isn't, however, educationally sound. This book provides ideas and strategies for making your classroom management easier. But remember: **The most critical variable in whether differentiation really happens is *your will* to make it happen.** Like other aspects of differentiated instruction, management becomes easier as your skills develop and your students become more independent.

How do I grade fairly if some students are doing more challenging work than others?

The way you grade or assign points to student work reflects your individual philosophy of evaluation. Ask yourself: Is the primary purpose of grades to give students feedback about their learning progress and the quality of their work? If so, then grades for differentiated assignments should reflect clearly stated criteria for quality work. A more challenging, complex task will have different criteria than a simpler, more basic task. However, the distinctions between criteria should reflect differences in the *kind* of work. Regardless of whether the differentiated activity is basic or advanced, you need to describe for students what "high quality" means for each specific task. Then you must fairly evaluate the product based on the criteria.

How can I make changes in the way I teach if I'm concerned that my school administration may not support differentiated instruction?

School administrators vary in their understanding of and commitment to differentiated learning. All administrators want their schools to be high performing, but they may not understand that for this to happen, teachers require training and time to develop strategies that will better meet students' needs.

Some administrators are concerned (as are teachers) about fairness issues. Will parents be alarmed about offering different kinds of learning activities to different students? Does offering different learning opportunities mean elitism? Exclusion? Preferential treatment?

You may want to provide information to administrators about how differentiated instruction helps teachers better implement standards-based education. Help them see the benefits of differentiated instruction in meeting the needs of a variety of learners in the inclusive classroom. Invite your principal in to see differentiation in action. Exhibit your students' products. Talk about how techniques of differentiated instruction make you a better teacher and your students better learners.

Figure 1 (page 18) summarizes the philosophy and practice of differentiation. Consider sharing this information with administrators, other teachers, or parents.

How can I make changes in the way I teach when we have no budget for training, materials, or resources?

Shrinking school budgets mean that funds for materials and resources, professional development, curriculum writing, and planning may be severely limited. Schools need to get creative to find the time and money necessary to make changes that lead to differentiation. What could happen in your school? Could a substitute be hired to move from class to class as teachers use part of their day for planning or training? As suggested earlier, could teachers within a department or grade level target specific curricular areas for differentiation, each take a unit or two, and then trade with each other? Could two teachers block time during a unit when one facilitates an activity with both classes while the other plans?

Differentiated instruction isn't a curriculum that requires the purchase of supplies. It's a way of thinking about your teaching and about the diversity of your students. Differentiated instruction is a collection of strategies that enables you to better address and manage the variety of learning needs in your classroom.

FIGURE 1

Differentiated Instruction Means . . .

- Recognizing the learning diversity represented in today's classrooms.

- Affirming that students have different learning needs, strengths, styles, interests, and preferences.

- Maintaining a commitment to curriculum standards and learning goals for all students.

- Increasing the variety in teaching, learning, and assessment in order to reach more students and respond to their preferences, styles, interests, and strengths.

- Providing high levels of challenge and active engagement in rigorous, relevant, and significant learning.

- Acknowledging what students already know and can do.

- Recognizing that students do not all need to do the same work in the same way.

- Diagnosing student needs and prescribing tasks that create better matches between students and their learning needs, styles, and/or preferences.

- Nurturing students' ability to make appropriate choices about how to learn and how to best present what they have learned.

- Designing differentiated (tiered) assignments to better respond to students' specific learning needs.

- Using flexible instructional grouping to provide opportunities for students to learn with others who have similar needs, styles, or preferences.

- Affirming the importance and value of all students' work.

- Creating fair and equitable processes for evaluating student learning and assigning grades.

How Differentiated Is Your Classroom?

Before you start to examine the strategies offered in this book, take some time to identify what elements of differentiation you already use. The following Classroom Practices Inventory (pages 19–20) will give you some idea about how well your current instructional strategies and classroom practices reflect the principles of differentiated instruction. As you respond to each inventory item, think about the ways you plan, teach, assess, and manage. Next, mark on the scale where you would place your practices. Are you closer to the characteristic in the right column or the one in the left? Few teachers are likely to use all characteristics of differentiated instruction (or all characteristics of traditional instruction, for that matter).

Classroom Practices Inventory

Use this inventory to look at what you are already doing in your classroom to differentiate instruction. Mark an "X" on each line to show where your current teaching practices lie on the continuum.

Traditional classroom: *Differentiated classroom:*

Covering the curriculum is my first   I base my teaching on students' learning
priority and directs my teaching.   needs as well as on the curriculum.

Learning goals remain the same for   Learning goals are adjusted for students
all students.   based on their needs.

I emphasize mastery of content and skills.   I emphasize critical and creative thinking
                                             and the application of learning.

Students use the same informational   I match students to specific informational
resources (books, articles, websites).   resources based on their learning needs
                                             and abilities.

I primarily use whole-class instruction.   I use several instructional formats
                                             (for example, whole class, small groups,
                                             partners, individuals).

I tend to group students heterogeneously.   As appropriate, I group students for
                                             instruction based on their learning needs.

All students move through the curricu-   The pace of instruction may vary, based
lum together and at the same pace.   on students' learning needs.

All students complete the same activities.   As appropriate, I give students oppor-
                                             tunities to choose activities based on
                                             their interests.

Continued ➡

Classroom Practices Inventory continued . . .

I tend to use similar instructional strategies day to day.	I use a variety of instructional strategies (for example, lectures, manipulatives, role plays, simulations, readings).
All students complete all activities.	Students complete different activities based on their needs or learning preferences.
All students are involved in all instructional activities.	I use methods for testing out of work and for compacting (speeding up, eliminating, replacing) work, as appropriate.
My enrichment work provides more content or more application of skills.	My enrichment work demands critical and/or creative thinking and the production of new ideas, thoughts, and perspectives.
In reteaching, I provide more practice using a similar instructional method.	In reteaching, I use a different instructional method from the one I used to teach the material the first time.
My reteaching activities typically involve lower-level thinking—knowledge and comprehension—to reinforce basic skills and content.	My reteaching activities demand higher-level thinking while reinforcing basic skills and content.
I assume that students have limited or no knowledge of curriculum content.	Before beginning a unit, I use preassessment strategies to determine what students already know.
I usually assess students' learning at the end of an instructional sequence.	I use ongoing assessment to check students' learning throughout an instructional sequence.
I typically use the same assessment tool, product, or project for all students.	I allow for learner differences by providing a variety of ways to show learning.

CHAPTER 2

Who Are Your Students?

The goal of differentiating instruction is to increase the likelihood that students will be successful learners. A good way to enhance students' chances for success is to get to know them and to understand how they differ from one another in interests, learning preferences and pace, readiness and motivation. How do you get to know your students so you can more successfully differentiate instruction for them?

Discovering Your Students

This chapter presents a number of tools for gathering information about your students' academic history, interests, preferred ways of learning, and current level of knowledge and skills. It isn't crucial that you use these tools at the beginning of the year—you can begin to differentiate instruction at any time. But the earlier you start gathering information, the more you'll have to draw on as you plan activities and units.

Academic History

Many teachers begin to gather information by reviewing students' academic histories. If your school maintains a cumulative file or portfolio on each student, this is a good place to find out about past performance. There you'll often find records of any standardized tests students have taken. While these scores may not tell you much about a student's specific skills and content knowledge, they can give you a sense of her or his academic strengths and limitations.* Compare a student's scores on standardized tests with grades and other performance assessments. Then ask yourself: Is this student doing as well as the scores suggest or is this student underachieving based on test results, grades, or both? If it appears that the student is underachieving, consider the possible underlying causes. Underachievement may stem from a mismatch between the student and the learning. Is the material too hard, too easy, or presented in a way that does not match the student's learning style and preferences? The information you gather using the tools in this chapter will help you think about learning matches and your students' success. Success in learning boosts academic self-confidence, which can help many students grow out of a cycle of school failure.[1]

A student's file or portfolio may also contain records of the basic skills tests or competency tests required by many states at particular grade levels. Such scores provide information about a student's present skill development. Results can indicate whether a student is making adequate progress toward meeting graduation requirements. When you differentiate instruction for students who have not met required levels of proficiency, you provide more opportunities for instruction and practice. When you differentiate instruction for students who have reached required competency levels, you allow them to proceed to more advanced learning.

If you're unable to obtain a student's academic history, perhaps because the student is new to your school or because a previous school didn't collect or transfer such information, you'll need to gather the data yourself. This might mean contacting the previous school or speaking to former teachers, or even talking with a parent or guardian who might have kept records of the student's past grades and/or scores on standardized and basic skills tests.

To organize and keep track of the information you collect, it may be helpful to create a profile sheet for each student (see the Student Learning Profile on pages 27–28). Use this profile to record evidence of past, current, and ongoing academic progress. The form includes room for noting any special learning needs or modifications, such as

---

*I prefer the word "limitation" to "weakness." A limitation suggests an area that is *currently* less developed. You can help your students strengthen these areas by encouraging them to use all of the intelligences, not just the ones they prefer.

[1] See *Up from Underachievement* by Diane Heacox (Minneapolis: Free Spirit Publishing, 1991).

those recommended by special education services or noted by previous teachers, as well as students' interests, learning preferences and styles, and multiple intelligences strengths. These are areas you may need to discover for yourself. Other tools in this chapter, such as the Interest Inventory (pages 29–31); How I Like to Learn (for younger grades) (pages 32–33); Projects, Presentations, Performances (pages 34–38); and Multiple Intelligences Checklist (pages 41–43) can help you. Add new information to students' profiles as you get to know them better. You may also find it useful to create a database of student information sorted by learning preferences, interests, and academic strengths and limitations.

Student Interests

To discover what interests your students both in and out of school, and how they see themselves as learners, ask them to fill out the Interest Inventory on pages 29–31. (Teachers of grades K–5 may need to make appropriate modifications on the form for use with their students.) Use this information to plan differentiated activities that respond to their specific interests. After the students have completed the inventory, hand out three index cards per student. Ask them to write their names at the top of each card, then:

1. On the first card, ask students to list the topics they rated as 1 or 2 on item 5 of the Interest Inventory. You can use these cards to create partners or teams with common or different interests.

2. On the second card, ask students to list one or more topics they'd like to learn about, based on their answers to item 7 on the Interest Inventory. Use these responses as a quick reference for grouping students to explore special topics.

3. On the third card, ask students to list the topics they know a lot about, based on their answers to item 13. Use these cards to determine "specialists" for particular areas of study.

Referring to items 19 and 20 in the inventory, note how students *prefer* to work and *how they believe they learn best*. This may be helpful

as you form partnerships or learning groups. You will have a sense of who most enjoys individual work, working with a partner, or working with a small group.

Multiple Intelligences

Another valuable way to get to know your students is through Howard Gardner's multiple intelligences model. As mentioned in Chapter 1 (page 7), Gardner's work has broadened our definition of what intelligence or "being smart" means. He suggests that there are at least nine "intelligences"—nine different ways of learning and thinking—and that each person has relative strengths and limitations among these. Gardner's model currently reflects eight affirmed intelligences and a ninth, the existential (2006), which he calls "tentative." Further research, including neurological research, needs to be conducted to fully verify its formal inclusion.

Students' strengths and preferences affect not only the ease with which they learn but also how they can best represent what they know and understand.

Gardner's nine intelligences are:

- verbal/linguistic
- logical/mathematical
- visual/spatial
- bodily/kinesthetic
- musical
- interpersonal
- intrapersonal
- naturalist
- existential[2]

See How We Think and Learn, page 40, for a description of each intelligence.

---

[2] *Multiple Intelligences: New Horizons* by Howard Gardner (New York: Basic Books, 2006).

Gardner's work can help you add variety to the ways you teach and the projects you assign. It can also help you get to know your students—for example, the ways they best learn and work, how they see themselves as learners, and how family members see them. This is all crucial information for matching individual students with the ways that they may learn best.

Interest Surveys

One way to get at students' interests and strengths is to have them complete an interest survey, like the How I Like to Learn survey for early primary grades (pages 32–33) or the Projects, Presentations, Performances survey (pages 34–35 for grades 3–5 or pages 36–38 for grades 6 and up).

On the How I Like to Learn survey, students circle the face that best represents their response for each of the 28 statements. The statements can be read to younger students or students can fill out the survey on their own. The key that follows tells which statement numbers correspond to each of Gardner's nine intelligences.

Key to How I Like to Learn responses:

Verbal/Linguistic: 1, 18, 22

Logical/Mathematical: 5, 16, 26

Visual/Spatial: 3, 8, 13

Bodily/Kinesthetic: 4, 11, 17, 27

Musical: 6, 12, 19

Interpersonal: 2, 15, 20

Intrapersonal: 10, 22, 28

Naturalist: 7, 9, 23

Existential: 14, 24, 25

For the Projects, Presentations, Performances survey, students read nine lists of products and circle those they'd prefer to do as a way to show what they've learned. Because students are not apt to circle activities they have not tried, such as designing a website, make it clear that they can choose a project even if they've never had an opportunity to do it in the past. Tell your students that the information from Projects, Presentations, Performances will help you know what kinds of things they like to do.

The nine lists correspond to Gardner's nine intelligences, although they aren't identified in that way. I've found that when the lists carry titles, students are more likely to classify themselves as verbal/linguistic or musical, rather than be open to all possibilities in all lists. If you prefer, you can list the projects in random order, rather than leave them "invisibly" classified by intelligence. If so, you'll need a key to identify each activity by its preferred intelligence.

The lists are organized as follows:

List 1 = Verbal/Linguistic

List 2 = Logical/Mathematical

List 3 = Visual/Spatial

List 4 = Bodily/Kinesthetic

List 5 = Musical

List 6 = Interpersonal

List 7 = Intrapersonal

List 8 = Naturalist

List 9 = Existential

Teaching About Multiple Intelligences

You'll find that many students, from elementary through high school, find information about the multiple intelligences very helpful. Kids appreciate insights into why some tasks are difficult for them while others are a breeze—and much more enjoyable. To some students, this is a big "Aha!" Knowing about multiple intelligences can also help students make good decisions when they're asked to decide how they will learn something or when they're given a choice of project.

Have your students complete the Projects, Presentations, Performances survey before you introduce them to Gardner's ideas. Then, to help explain these concepts to students, pass out copies and discuss About Multiple Intelligences, page 39, and How We Think and Learn, page 40. Mention that each intelligence is not necessarily used all by itself. Sometimes what we're asked to learn is presented in a way that calls on more than one way of thinking. A project or product often requires more than one kind of intelligence to complete. For example, to understand an idea, we first may need to read about it (verbal/linguistic intelligence) and then construct a chart or graphic organizer explaining it (logical/mathematical and possibly visual/spatial intelligence).

Ask your student to review their Projects, Presentations, Performances survey and note which lists had the greatest numbers of circles. Provide each list's title. Make sure your students understand that the purpose of the survey is to provide more information on their product preferences. Make it clear that it is not your intention to label students, nor should students conclude that one way of thinking is preferable to others. Emphasize that all individuals have particular learning strengths and limitations. Mention that we can strengthen our ability to use all the intelligences by being patient with ourselves.

Put This into Action

Assign a color to each of the nine intelligences. Using index cards, draw or affix colored dots in the upper right corner of each card (for example, cards with red dots might mean bodily/kinesthetic). Based on the results of Projects, Presentations, Performances, have each student select the cards that reflect their top two strengths. Ask students to write their name on each card. Collect the cards and use the color codes to sort students into groups or partnerships for various purposes:

■ To match students to particular activities.

■ To form learning teams of students with similar strengths.

■ To form learning teams of students with different strengths.

Involving Families

Since parents and other family members see our students in unique ways, it can be valuable to solicit their perceptions about kids' preferences and characteristics. The Multiple Intelligences Checklist (pages 41–43) asks families for their perspective on their student's interests and learning preferences. Like students, families

appreciate information on Gardner's theory of multiple intelligences. It's reassuring to know that the concept of intelligence has broadened to include many more strengths than the traditional IQ score reveals.

You'll want to accompany the checklist with a letter explaining its purposes, how the information will be used, and its potential benefits for students. (See page 47 for a sample letter.) If possible, send the letter and checklist at the beginning of the school year, asking families to return it by a particular date or to bring it to fall conferences. But don't let the time of year stop you. This information will be valuable regardless of when you decide to gather it.

Each item on the checklist corresponds to one of the nine intelligences, but it's better not to include specific information about items until parents have completed the form. Knowing that an item suggests logical/mathematical intelligence, for example, may influence a response.

Use the answer key on pages 44–46 to analyze the checklists, and determine three areas of greatest preference for each student. You may wish to send the results home with a letter of explanation (see page 48 for a sample letter) and a copy of About Multiple Intelligences (page 39) and How We Think and Learn (page 40) to help families understand more about the results.

Multiple Intelligences Observations

The Multiple Intelligences Observations grids (see pages 49–57) can be used to record your own observations about students. Think about each of Gardner's nine intelligences and ask yourself: Which of my students has these characteristics? List your students' names on the numbered lines. Moving across each row, check the characteristics that seem applicable to each student, based on your observations. Or go down each column, considering each characteristic in turn. Complete these grids once you've had an opportunity to observe your students or fill them out gradually over the course of the year.

Keep in mind that all the tools provided in this chapter are intended to provide *perspectives* on preferred thinking and learning styles, not to test, label, or categorize students. Gardner suggests that intelligences are best revealed by observing students engaged in learning. There are no particular paper-and-pencil tests for multiple intelligences. The purpose of the various forms and checklists is to help you gather information to better respond to learners' needs as you plan differentiated instruction.

Finding Out What Students Know

As we've seen, increasing the likelihood of student success means knowing where your students are on the learning continuum so you can modify and adjust your plans to respond to their needs. Here are several ways to find out what students know.

Preassessments and Pretests

Teachers often preassess or pretest students on particular skills or content knowledge. Preassessment is particularly important when you're differentiating curriculum based on what students already know and what they need to learn.

Students who show proficiency, as demonstrated by a particular score on a pretest, can move on to activities that extend or enrich their learning. Those who need additional instruction and practice get extra time.

Many math and language arts textbooks include skill pretests. If pretests are not available from your textbook publisher, selected textbook exercises or unit tests can serve as pretests. Pretest information is also found by reading records and skill mastery charts. If you use ongoing assessment, you may have student portfolios with pretest records that suggest what individual students have mastered or need to work on.

KW: Know, Want to Know

KWL is the acronym for an instructional strategy that many teachers use both before and after an activity or unit. It stands for: What do I *know* about this topic? What do I *want to know* about the topic? What did I *learn*? The KW parts of the strategy give valuable information for differentiating instruction; the K suggests students' current knowledge of a topic and the W captures their interests and degree of curiosity.

You might say to your class, "Let's find out what you know about nutrition," and then map or list their ideas on the board. This information will suggest content that you may want to adjust or even eliminate if most students know it.

You can also ask students to respond on paper. In that case, you'll have more specific information about what each individual knows about the topic. Students can then use their responses to contribute to a class discussion of the topic.

You may notice that a few students know quite a bit about a topic, a few know very little, while most students are likely to have knowledge somewhere in the middle. All groups are likely candidates for differentiated tasks. Think through how you will provide basic information for students who need it without requiring unnecessary review for more proficient students.

Next, ask students, "What do you want to learn about nutrition?" Record those ideas or have students record their questions individually. Now you'll see ways to tailor the unit to your students' interests. KW is an informal, on-your-feet preassessment that gives you a feel for the range of needs and interests in your classroom.

Your Grade Book or Class Record

Your grade book or class record can be a useful resource both for identifying students' learning needs and for helping you form instructional groups. As you record grades or points, note at the top of each column the particular skill or area of content that was assessed. For example, if the score relates to the ability to write a hypothesis, note this. Then, if you want to form instructional groups based on learning needs, simply read down the columns using a predetermined mastery level to see who has and hasn't achieved mastery. Your groups for reteaching are easily revealed.

For example, if you're setting up a science lab that requires hypothesis writing, your records will tell you who needs more practice and who is ready to move on to the lab. Those who can write hypotheses will begin the lab; those who cannot will stay with you for further instruction.

Professional Observations

Don't underestimate what you know about your students' current level of learning based on your observations in the classroom. Preassessment information can come from more than paper-and-pencil activities or performance packages. You probably have a good sense about who has mastered skills or content simply by paying attention to students' responses in discussions, observing small-group activities, and doing over-the-shoulder reviews of individual work. Such informal assessments can help you determine the general need for differentiated activities. It can also alert you to particular students or groups of students who would benefit either from more time and practice or more advanced learning opportunities.

Conferences

Parents and other family members often have valuable information about students' skills and interests. The kinds of activities that students engage in at home, in their neighborhoods, and in their community offer insights that may help you in differentiating instruction.

Conferences are good times to get more information about individual students. If you have the results of the Interest Inventory or Multiple Intelligences Checklist, you may wish to share this information with parents. As time allows, you might discuss how the information can help you work with the student.

Structure your conversation with parents to allow you to gather information that can help you in differentiating instruction. Pose questions such as:

What's going well for _____?

What's difficult for him or her?

What was a high point for _____ this semester?

What concerns do you have about _____'s progress in school?

If you have difficulty getting family members to attend conferences, you could include these questions in a letter. Ask parents either to email or mail responses to you (enclose a postage-paid envelope) or to discuss them with you as part of a telephone conference. You might also have these questions available for parents to think about as they wait for their conference to start. Family members may feel more comfortable talking with you if you give them the opportunity to think through some topics in advance. You'll also be helping ensure that the limited time available for conferences is used for the student's greatest benefit.

The Importance of Knowing Your Students

Differentiating instruction begins with knowing your students and their learning needs. Review what is readily available to you: academic history, test results, your grade book, your professional observations, students' work portfolios. Gather additional information through student inventories, preassessments, and family conferences and conversations. Now that you know more about your students, you're ready to look at your curriculum. What do you want to teach your students? That's the topic of Chapter 3.

Student Learning Profile

Name: _____

ACHIEVEMENT TEST

Name of test: _____

	Year	Previous Year	Current Grades
Math (overall)			
_____ (subtest)			
_____ (subtest)			
Science			
Social Studies			
Language Arts (overall)			
_____ (subtest)			
_____ (subtest)			
Reading (overall)			
_____ (subtest)			
_____ (subtest)			

APTITUDE AND/OR INTELLIGENCE TEST

Name of test: _____

	Year	National Percentile Score	Local Percentile Score
Verbal			
Spatial			
Quantitative			

Continued ➡

Student Learning Profile continued . . .

GRADES

	Previous Year	Current Grades
Language Arts/English		
Mathematics		
Social Studies		
Science		
Other areas:		

Notes on results of state assessments:

_____

_____

Special learning needs or modifications (including special education recommendations):

_____

Interests:

_____

Prefers to work: ❏ alone   ❏ with partner   ❏ in small group   ❏ in large group

Learning profile notes:

_____

Multiple intelligences strengths/preferences (Verbal/Linguistic, Musical, Logical/Mathematical, Interpersonal, Visual/Spatial, Intrapersonal, Bodily/Kinesthetic, Naturalist, Existential):

_____

_____

Comments:_____

Interest Inventory

Name:_____ Date:_____

1. **What is your favorite activity or subject in school? Why? Your least favorite? Why?**

2. **What are your "best" subjects? What makes them the easiest for you?**

3. **What subjects are difficult for you? What makes them the hardest?**

4. **What subject makes you think and work the hardest? Why is it the most challenging?**

5. **Rate the following topics according to your interests.**
   (1 = very interested, 2 = somewhat interested, 3 = not interested)

   ___ Dance   ___ Music
   ___ Drama   ___ Sports
   ___ Writing   ___ Math
   ___ Computers   ___ Science
   ___ Social Studies   ___ Business
   ___ World Languages ___ Politics/Law

6. **What are your favorite games or sports?**

7. **If you could learn about anything you wanted to, what would you choose to learn about? Be specific.** (For example: science-fiction writing, meteorology, architecture, Shakespeare, Africa.)

8. What are three things you like to *do* when you have free time (besides seeing friends)?

9. What clubs, groups, teams, or organizations do you belong to? Include both school activities and those not sponsored by the school.

10. What things have you collected in the past? What, if anything, are you currently collecting?

11. Have you ever taught yourself to do something without the help of another person? If so, what?

12. If you were going to start a book club, what kinds of books would your club read?

13. If people were to come to you for information about something you know a lot about, what would the topic be?

14. If you could plan a field trip for learning, where would you go? Why would you choose that place?

15. When you're using the computer, are you usually playing games, doing homework, doing research, visiting websites, visiting chat rooms, social networking, shopping, exchanging email, programming, or some other activity?

Continued ➡

Interest Inventory continued . . .

16. **If you could interview an expert on any subject, what subject would you like to talk to someone about?**

17. **If you could interview one significant person from the present and one from the past, who would you interview? Why would you choose these two people?**

18. **What careers are you currently interested in?**

19. **In school, I *prefer* to work:**
    ❑ alone   ❑ with one other person   ❑ in a small group   ❑ in a larger group

20. **In school, I *learn* best:**
    ❑ alone   ❑ with one other person   ❑ in a small group   ❑ in a larger group

21. **What helps you learn?** (For example, a hands-on activity, reading, taking notes, or reading out loud.)

22. **What makes learning more difficult for you?** (For example, lectures, lots of writing.)

23. **Think of a great teacher you've had. Describe what made this teacher so terrific.**

24. **What past school assignment or project are you proudest of? Why?**

25. **What project done outside of school are you proudest of? Why?**

26. **What else would you like me to know about you as a learner?**

Adapted from *The Interest-A-Lyzer*, by J.S. Renzulli (Mansfield Center, CT: Creative Learning Press, 1997). Used with permission.

How I Like to Learn

My Name:_____

1. I like reading books and stories.	☺	☺	😐
2. I like working with others.	☺	☺	☺
3. I like to draw.	☺	☺	☺
4. I like dancing and/or sports.	☺	☺	☺
5. I like numbers and counting. I like math.	☺	☺	😐
6. I like making music.	☺	☺	😐
7. I have a collection of things that are special to me.	☺	☺	☺
8. I like putting together puzzles.	☺	☺	😐
9. I like to solve problems.	☺	☺	☺
10. I like making decisions for myself.	☺	☺	😐
11. I like pretending, acting things out, or playing dress up.	☺	☺	☺
12. I remember songs.	☺	☺	😐
13. I like to do art projects and make things.	☺	☺	😐
14. I like to help people.	☺	☺	☺
15. I would rather work with other people than work on my own.	☺	☺	😐

32

How I Like to Learn continued . . .

	😀	🙂	😐
16. I will work on a problem or puzzle until I figure it out.			
17. I like to build things with blocks or Legos.			
18. I like to write or tell stories.			
19. I can play a musical instrument.			
20. I like to be the leader.			
21. I am not afraid to tell people what I think.			
22. I like riddles, rhymes, and poems.			
23. I like to figure out how things work.			
24. I want to hear the ideas of other people.			
25. I am concerned about the feelings of other people.			
26. I like doing math puzzles or brain teasers.			
27. I like to do science experiments.			
28. I like to think carefully about something before I do it.			

Projects, Presentations, Performances (Grades 3–5)

Name:_____

What kinds of school assignments or projects do you like to do? Read the following nine lists. For each list, draw a circle around all the different activities you would enjoy doing to show others what you've learned.

List 1 _____

Debating	Doing creative writing	Writing a letter to the editor	Creating an acrostic poem
Writing poetry	Creating a riddle	Writing a fairy tale, fable, folktale, or tall tale	Writing an email or text message
Making a speech	Writing a report	Creating a newspaper or magazine	Creating a word collage using wordle.net
Storytelling	Creating a crossword puzzle		
Writing an essay	Writing a journal	Writing a letter	Developing a sales pitch or commercial
Writing a research paper	Writing a summary	Creating a nursery rhyme	Scripting a newscast
Writing a story	Writing a pamphlet or brochure	Constructing a flipbook	Creating a tongue twister
Writing a biography		Creating a podcast	Participating in an online discussion
Writing a magazine or newspaper article	Writing a slogan	Writing a book or movie review	
	Writing a conversation or dialogue		

List 2 _____

Designing a maze or puzzle	Constructing a T chart (+, -)	Recording information on a chart	Creating a graphic organizer
Investigating a problem	Making a flowchart		Developing a hypothesis
Making an outline	Constructing a timeline	Designing a survey	Creating a scale drawing
Solving math problems	Constructing a chart or graph	Using Kidspiration software to create fact maps	Completing logic puzzles
Making a diagram		Designing a computer program, game, or graphics	Constructing a Venn diagram
Creating a fact web	Inventing a code		

List 3 _____

Drawing	Making a collage	Creating a board game	Creating a digital animation
Sketching	Making visual aids for a presentation (graphics, props)	Creating a photo essay	Making a diorama
Painting		Designing a pamphlet or brochure	Creating a PowerPoint presentation
Designing a Web page	Taking photographs	Designing a bumper sticker	Designing a billboard
Creating a pop-up book	Making a mobile	Designing a logo	Writing a graphic novel or short story
Creating a cartoon or comic strip	Making a storyboard	Designing a postcard	
Making a clay sculpture	Designing a structure or building	Creating a picture book	Creating a wordless book
Making a map		Designing a greeting card	Creating a digital montage of images and music
Making a poster	Making a diagram	Making a digital movie	
Making a mural	Creating illustrations for an ad	Designing sets for a play	

Continued ➡

List 4

Role-playing

Making a video

Performing a skit

Pantomiming

Doing a demonstration

Constructing a 3-D model

Making a digital movie

Creating new strategies for a sport

Performing a dance or other creative movement

Performing in a play

Constructing a model

Creating something to post on YouTube

Building or taking apart something

Developing an invention

Doing a science experiment

Playing interactive games

Using manipulatives in math

List 5

Performing music

Composing lyrics to an existing melody

Performing or writing a rap

Creating a jingle

Creating a slogan

Finding digital music to illustrate an idea

Writing a song

Writing a limerick

Creating digital music

Finding patterns

Creating digital sounds

Singing in a group, choir, or chorus

Playing a musical instrument

Performing rhythms with a percussion instrument

Creating a digital montage of images and music

List 6

Participating in a group activity/project

Participating in a discussion

Conducting an interview

Doing collaborative work

Engaging in an online discussion

Debating personal thoughts, ideas, perspectives

Solving problems with a group

Planning a campaign for a cause or an issue

Contributing to a message board to share your ideas

Doing a volunteer project with others

Organizing an event or activity

List 7

Keeping a personal journal

Setting personal goals

Expressing your opinions and ideas

Considering your beliefs about something

Taking online surveys or inventories

Sharing your opinions and perspectives in online discussions

Contributing to a message board to state your opinions

Sharing your opinion in a blog

Keeping a personal log or record

List 8

Classifying objects

Making predictions

Identifying objects based on their characteristics

Creating a collection

Solving a problem

Sorting and organizing objects

Identifying likenesses and differences

Participating in virtual fieldtrips

Constructing a display of objects or artifacts

Making comparisons

Planning a walking tour

Creating a guidebook

Designing an exhibit

Investigating how something works

Making observations

Identifying a problem

Participating in an in-class or online simulation

List 9

Exploring theories and ideas

Considering the fairness of an issue

Solving moral dilemmas

Helping other people

Examining your personal beliefs and viewpoints

Comparing and contrasting beliefs and viewpoints

Considering the effects on the environment

Considering the effects on others

Studying philosophy or religions

Working on a project to solve a community problem or make something better

Working on a campaign or fundraiser for a community group

Projects, Presentations, Performances (Grades 6 & up)

Name:_____

What kinds of school assignments or projects do you like to do? Read the following nine lists. For each list, draw a circle around all the different activities you would enjoy doing to show others what you've learned.

List 1

Writing a character sketch

Debating

Writing poetry

Making a speech

Storytelling

Writing an essay

Writing a research paper

Writing a story

Writing a biography

Writing a magazine or newspaper article

Designing a checklist

Writing fiction or nonfiction

Writing a report

Making an audio recording

Creating sales pitch or commercial

Writing a journal

Writing a summary

Writing a pamphlet or brochure

Creating a slogan or motto

Writing a conversation or dialogue

Writing a letter to the editor

Taking part in a mock trial

Writing an information brief

Creating a newspaper or magazine

Writing an epitaph

Writing a fable, myth, or legend

Creating a satire or spoof

Creating a book or movie review

Composing an email or text message

Writing an ode or sonnet

Scripting a newscast

Creating a monologue

Writing an epilogue

Creating a narrative poem

Creating word collages using wordle.net

Creating a podcast

List 2

Designing a maze or puzzle

Investigating a problem

Making an outline

Designing a matrix

Making a diagram

Creating an analogy

Critiquing an event or product

Constructing a timeline

Constructing a chart or graph

Solving logic problems

Creating a T-chart (+ , -)

Recording data on a chart

Calculating probabilities

Developing a theory

Making a calculation

Analyzing trends and patterns

Developing a formula

Computing an answer

Inventing a code

Making a storyboard

Solving an equation or number problem

Doing an evaluation or a rating

Recording data or information

Doing an analysis

Drawing a caricature

Doing a critique

Constructing a flowchart

Doing a scale drawing

Creating a spreadsheet

Designing a Webquest

Designing and analyzing an opinion poll or a survey

Designing a computer program, game, or graphic

Developing a hypothesis

Formulating plans

Testing theories

Creating a graphic organizer

Testing hypotheses

Analyzing ideas

Using Inspiration software to create fact webs

Continued ➡

Projects, Presentations, Performances (Grades 6 & up) continued . . .

List 3

Drawing, sketching, or painting

Illustrating

Building a prototype

Designing a Web page

Creating a cartoon or comic strip

Making a clay sculpture

Writing a graphic novel or short story

Designing a logo

Making a map

Making a poster

Making a mural

Making a collage

Making visual aids for a presentation (graphics, props)

Taking photographs

Constructing a scrapbook

Mapping ideas

Designing a postcard

Creating a PowerPoint presentation

Making a mobile

Constructing a model

Designing a structure

Making a diagram

Planning advertising graphics

Taking photos

Photoshopping

Constructing a display of a collection

Designing a photo essay

Creating digital animation

Creating a board game

Designing a pamphlet or brochure

Designing a greeting card

Designing sets for a play

Creating a digital montage of images and music

List 4

Role-playing

Dramatizing

Performing a skit

Pantomiming

Creating something to post on YouTube

Creating digital movies

Using digital probes

Performing a dance or other creative movement

Doing improvisational acting

Engaging in interactive games

Performing in a play

Constructing a model

Making a video recording

Doing a parody, spoof, or satire

Doing hands-on activities

Building or taking apart something

Developing an invention

Doing a lab activity or an experiment

Conducting a demonstration

List 5

Performing music

Composing lyrics

Performing in a musical

Creating digital sounds

Identifying patterns

Creating a slogan

Planning a multi-media presentation

Creating a limerick

Identifying digital music to convey a feeling or illustrate an idea

Performing or writing a rap

Creating a jingle

Performing rhythms with a percussion instrument

Writing a song

Singing in a group, choir, or chorus

Playing a musical instrument

Writing music

Improvising music

Creating a digital montage of images and music

List 6

Participating in a group activity

Participating in a discussion

Conducting an interview

Engaging in an online discussion

Sharing your ideas on a message board

Debating personal thoughts, ideas, perspectives

Building consensus within a group

Solving problems with a group

Planning a campaign for a cause or an issue

Participating in a roundtable discussion

Organizing an event or activity

Helping with conflict resolution

Doing peer counseling

Paraphrasing ideas of others

Continued ➡

Projects, Presentations, Performances (Grades 6 & up) continued . . .

List 7

Keeping a personal journal or diary

Keeping a personal log or record

Sharing your perspectives or viewpoints through an online discussion

Setting personal goals

Completing online surveys or inventories

Sharing your opinions on a message board

Sharing your opinion on a blog

Developing a critical review

Developing an investigative report

Summarizing your ideas or beliefs

Identifying your beliefs about an issue

Making a self-assessment of your work

Developing a policy statement

Developing a critique

Developing support for a personal opinion

Presenting your personal viewpoint, perspective, or belief

List 8

Classifying objects

Identifying problems

Making predictions

Solving problems

Identifying objects based on characteristics

Conducting observations

Creating a guidebook

Exploring a topic or theme

Creating a collection

Participating in an in-class or online simulation

Constructing a display of objects or artifacts

Making comparisons

Planning a walking tour

Investigating how something works

Designing an exhibit

Creating a database

Charting hierarchies and connections

Mapping ideas

Engaging in virtual fieldtrips

Identifying common traits

Sorting and organizing objects or ideas

Ranking things by significance or importance

List 9

Examining philosophical beliefs

Exploring theoretical models

Resolving moral dilemmas

Considering the ethics of an issue

Analyzing opposing beliefs

Examining personal beliefs, viewpoints, or perspectives

Comparing and contrasting opposing beliefs, viewpoints, or perspectives

Identifying philosophical themes

Investigating philosophical and religious issues

Examining the underlying meanings of historical events

Considering the effects of actions on the environment

Considering the effects of actions on others

Examining multiple points of view on an issue or idea

Helping other people

Working on a project to solve a community problem or make something better

Working on a campaign or fundraiser for a community group

About Multiple Intelligences

Important things to remember about multiple intelligences

- Educational professor Howard Gardner has explored nine ways to think and learn—so far. There are probably more to be discovered.

- You are stronger in some areas (intelligences) than others. But everyone has strengths and limitations.

- There is no one best way to learn. All are important.

- You may find that learning comes easier or is more fun in your areas of strength.

- You need experiences in all nine ways of thinking so you can "pump up" the ones you're less strong in.

- Many things you do require you to use more than one intelligence to accomplish a task.

- Multiple intelligences aren't meant to label you. They're simply information about your learning preferences.

How you can use multiple intelligences

- Information about your preferences can help you make good choices when you're asked to decide how you'll learn something or when you're given a choice of project.

- Thinking about your strengths can give you ideas on how you might study more effectively. For example, if you're strong in visual/spatial thinking, drawing sketches or pictures may help you learn and remember.

- A group project can turn out well if the people in your group have different strengths. You may want to divide up tasks so that each member is working in a strength area. For example, the person who's strong in verbal/linguistic thinking does the writing, the person strong in visual/spatial thinking does the drawings or illustrations, and so on. Your project may be more successful if everyone gets to work in a way he or she prefers.

- A group project can also turn out well when all the people in your group have similar strengths. Think how good a skit could be if everyone in the group was strong in bodily/kinesthetic thinking!

- Working in a way that's harder for you will be more of a stretch. But you can still do high-quality work. Don't use multiple intelligence theory as an excuse for not doing your best.

How We Think and Learn

Say It. *Verbal/linguistic learners* enjoy and understand oral and written language. They prefer to communicate with others through speaking and writing. They often like to read. They learn best through language: listening, speaking, reading, telling, discussing, and writing.

Count It. *Logical/mathematical learners* love numbers of all sorts—numbers in math, naturally, but also the numbers associated with science, social studies, and language arts. The percentage of sea animals in each phyla, the population growth of the United States since the last census, the number of hours Americans spend watching television: these numbers will capture the attention of logical/mathematical learners. These learners have the ability to think conceptually and to see patterns. They like to solve problems and reason things out. They learn best using numbers and analysis.

Picture It. *Visual/spatial learners* make mental pictures and images to help themselves learn and remember. They learn best when material is represented visually such as in graphic organizers, pictures, webs, and diagrams.

Move It. *Bodily/kinesthetic learners* like to express themselves and their ideas through movement. They have good large-muscle and/or fine-motor skills and need to touch and do things. They learn best through action, hands-on activities, and the opportunity to manipulate materials.

Hum It. *Musical learners* respond to pitch, rhythm, and tone. They can easily see and identify patterns. They have a heightened listening ability. They may enjoy singing, rapping, or playing an instrument. They may or may not have musical skills, but they respond strongly to music. They learn best when learning is linked to their sense of patterning, rhythm, and music.

Lead It. *Interpersonal learners* are "people people." They are often good at motivating others, organizing, and communicating. They tend to get along well with others. Many are empathetic and intuitive. An interpersonal learner might use her leadership abilities as a student council member or as an organizer of a food drive. Another interpersonal learner might enjoy "stirring things up" a little. Students with an interpersonal preference enjoy working and learning with others.

Reflect on It. *Intrapersonal learners* are thoughtful and reflective. They closely examine ideas, issues, and perspectives. They understand themselves and their own feelings about things. They like their independence and may set goals to work toward. For them, learning encompasses feelings, values, and attitudes. They learn best when allowed to reflect, share personal opinions, and work alone.

Investigate It. *Naturalist learners* can adjust to, adapt, and use their surroundings to succeed or survive. Some may be called "street smart." They observe how systems work and can be effective manipulators of situations and settings. They learn through examining classifications, categories, and hierarchies. They prefer that learning is connected to the real world. They learn best when called on to figure out how things work, to observe, and to investigate.

Investigate It. *Existentialist learners* (tentative, 2006) have the ability to contemplate big ideas. They are analytical. They have an explicit concern with spiritual or religious matters. They ponder the "human condition" and question the significance of life and the meaning of death. They are concerned about both our physical world (Earth) as well as the world of thoughts and feelings. They look for connections and relationships as they learn. They are passionate individuals who can become immersed in the arts. They learn best when asked to consider the "big questions"; explore philosophical, moral, or ethical aspects of issues; and engage in activities to serve "others" or to address social and political causes.

Adapted from the ideas of Howard Gardner. See his *Multiple Intelligences: New Horizons* (New York: Basic Books, 2006).

Multiple Intelligences Checklist

Student's name:_____

Your input will help me better understand your child. There are no right or wrong answers. Please check the items you believe most accurately describe your child.

_____ **1.** Demonstrates balance, small- and large-motor dexterity, and precision in physical tasks.

_____ **2.** Is very interested in math.

_____ **3.** Remembers melodies.

_____ **4.** Is highly observant of surroundings.

_____ **5.** Loves to chart, graph, map, and organize information.

_____ **6.** Enjoys examining philosophical and/or religious issues.

_____ **7.** Loves to tell stories and engage in conversation and discussion.

_____ **8.** Asks questions about fairness; has a strong interest in right and wrong, justice and injustice.

_____ **9.** Asks questions to seek more information about what she or he observes.

_____ **10.** Prefers to work independently; is self-directed.

_____ **11.** Shows mechanical skill; can take things apart and put them back together easily.

_____ **12.** Enthusiastically engages in service to others (fundraising, supporting issues of fairness and equity, volunteerism).

_____ **13.** Spells accurately and easily.

_____ **14.** Is well coordinated and has a good sense of timing.

_____ **15.** Has leadership abilities; is able to influence others' opinions and action.

_____ **16.** Easily computes math problems mentally.

_____ **17.** Is highly verbal and is able to clearly convey ideas orally.

_____ **18.** Plays a musical instrument with ease and/or has a good singing voice.

_____ **19.** Enjoys working on logic puzzles or brainteasers.

_____ **20.** Understands abstract ideas.

_____ **21.** Likes to move around and stay active.

_____ **22.** Draws and sketches accurately and with detail.

_____ **23.** Exhibits a high level of care and concern for others.

_____ **24.** Improvises vocal or instrumental music and/or composes music.

_____ **25.** Is able to adapt and adjust to changing circumstances; is flexible.

_____ **26.** Develops physical skills quickly and easily.

_____ **27.** Is fascinated and challenged by computers; easily uses computers for more than playing simple games.

Multiple Intelligences Checklist continued . . .

_____ **28.** Is sensitive to the feelings, thoughts, and motivations of others.

_____ **29.** Prefers things to be orderly and logical.

_____ **30.** Is "street smart"; understands how systems work and can use them to personal advantage.

_____ **31.** Enjoys acting things out, doing skits and plays; is dramatic.

_____ **32.** Has a good memory for names, places, dates, and other facts.

_____ **33.** Can mimic others' gestures or mannerisms.

_____ **34.** Is able to compare and contrast opposing beliefs, viewpoints, or perspectives.

_____ **35.** Likes to sketch out ideas or represent them visually.

_____ **36.** Excels in sports or other physical activities (dancing, martial arts, creative movement).

_____ **37.** Can easily identify, categorize, and classify objects, information, and ideas.

_____ **38.** Prefers to work and learn with others.

_____ **39.** Enjoys word games such as crossword puzzles, Scrabble, and acrostics.

_____ **40.** Exhibits high levels of concern for global, environmental issues.

_____ **41.** Understands cause and effect, actions and consequences.

_____ **42.** Has a strong will.

_____ **43.** Shows a strong interest in music.

_____ **44.** Accurately identifies and conveys feelings.

_____ **45.** Interacts comfortably and confidently with others.

_____ **46.** Is able to examine multiple points of view or perspectives.

_____ **47.** Learns best by seeing and observing; recalls information through images and pictures.

_____ **48.** Is comfortable with his or her individuality, regardless of peer pressure.

_____ **49.** Easily conveys thoughts and ideas in writing.

_____ **50.** Is interested in and sensitive to nature.

_____ **51.** Has a good vocabulary in comparison to age peers.

_____ **52.** Likes to read and do research to find out about topics of interest.

_____ **53.** Is fascinated with numbers and statistics (for example, baseball averages); has an excellent memory for such figures.

_____ **54.** Is able to organize and motivate others.

_____ **55.** Shows a strong sense of rhythm in movement and speech.

_____ **56.** Enjoys puzzles, mazes, and other visual challenges.

_____ **57.** Raises questions related to ethics or morals.

_____ **58.** Has a strong sense of self; high self-esteem.

Continued ➡

Multiple Intelligences Checklist continued . . .

_____ **59.** Often sings or hums.

_____ **60.** Reflects on and ponders situations.

_____ **61.** Prefers to be actively engaged with a subject, rather than simply hear or read about it.

_____ **62.** Enjoys chess, checkers, and other strategy games.

_____ **63.** Recognizes and understands her or his personal strengths and limitations.

_____ **64.** Likes making models and three-dimensional figures (for example, LEGO structures).

_____ **65.** Forms friendships easily.

_____ **66.** Questions the "fairness" of actions and incidents.

Adapted from the ideas of Howard Gardner. See his *Multiple Intelligences: New Horizons* (New York: Basic Books, 2006).

Answer Key for "Multiple Intelligences Checklist"

VL = Verbal/Linguistic   LM = Logical/Mathematical   VS = Visual/Spatial
BK = Bodily/Kinesthetic   M = Musical   IP = Interpersonal
IR = Intrapersonal   N = Naturalist   E = Existential

BK	1. Demonstrates balance, small- and large-motor dexterity, and precision in physical tasks.
LM	2. Is very interested in math.
M	3. Remembers melodies.
N	4. Is highly observant of surroundings.
LM	5. Loves to chart, graph, map, and organize information.
E	6. Enjoys examining philosophical and/or religious issues.
VL	7. Loves to tell stories and engage in conversations and discussions.
IR & IP	8. Asks questions about fairness; has a strong interest in right and wrong, justice and injustice.
N	9. Asks questions to seek more information about what she or he observes.
IR	10. Prefers to work independently; is self-directed.
VS & LM	11. Shows mechanical skill; can take things apart and put them back together easily.
E	12. Enthusiastically engages in service to others (fundraising, supporting issues of fairness and equity, volunteerism).
VL	13. Spells accurately and easily.
BK	14. Is well coordinated and has a good sense of timing.
IP	15. Has leadership abilities; is able to influence others' opinions and actions.
LM	16. Easily computes math problems mentally.
VL	17. Is highly verbal and is able to clearly convey ideas orally.
M	18. Plays a musical instrument with ease and/or has a good singing voice.
LM & N	19. Enjoys working on logic puzzles or brainteasers.
LM	20. Understands abstract ideas.
BK	21. Likes to move around and stay active.
VS	22. Draws and sketches accurately and with detail.
E	23. Exhibits a high level of care and concern for others.
M	24. Improvises vocal or instrumental music and/or composes music.
N	25. Is able to adapt and adjust to changing circumstances; is flexible.

Continued ➡

BK	26. Develops physical skills quickly and easily.
LM & VS	27. Is fascinated and challenged by computers; easily uses computers for more than playing simple games.
IR & IP	28. Is sensitive to the feelings, thoughts, and motivations of others.
LM	29. Prefers things to be orderly and logical.
N	30. Is "street smart"; understands how systems work and can use them to personal advantage.
BK	31. Enjoys acting things out, doing skits and plays; is dramatic.
N & VL	32. Has a good memory for names, places, dates, and other facts.
BK	33. Can mimic others' gestures or mannerisms.
E	34. Is able to compare and contrast opposing beliefs, viewpoints, or perspectives.
VS	35. Likes to sketch out ideas or represent them visually.
BK	36. Excels in sports or other physical activities (dancing, martial arts, creative movement).
N	37. Can easily identify, categorize, and classify objects, information, and ideas.
IP	38. Prefers to work and learn with others.
VL	39. Enjoys word games such as crossword puzzles, Scrabble, and acrostics.
E	40. Exhibits high levels of concern for global, environmental issues.
LM	41. Understands cause and effect, actions and consequences.
IR	42. Has a strong will.
M	43. Shows a strong interest in music.
IR	44. Accurately identifies and conveys feelings.
IP	45. Interacts comfortably and confidently with others.
E	46. Is able to examine multiple points of view or perspectives.
VS	47. Learns best by seeing and observing; recalls information through images and pictures.
IR	48. Is comfortable with his or her individuality, regardless of peer pressure.
VL	49. Easily conveys thoughts and ideas in writing.
N	50. Is interested in and sensitive to nature.
VL	51. Has a good vocabulary in comparison to age peers.
VL	52. Likes to read and do research to find out about topics of interest.
LM	53. Is fascinated with numbers and statistics (for example, baseball averages); has an excellent memory for such figures.

Continued ➡

IP	54. Is able to organize and motivate others.
M	55. Shows a strong sense of rhythm in movement and speech.
VS	56. Enjoys puzzles, mazes, and other visual challenges.
E	57. Raises questions related to ethics or morals.
IR	58. Has a strong sense of self.
M	59. Often sings or hums.
IR	60. Reflects on and ponders situations.
BK	61. Prefers to be actively engaged with a subject, rather than simply hear or read about it.
LM	62. Enjoys chess, checkers, and other strategy games.
IR	63. Recognizes and understands her or his personal strengths and limitations.
VS	64. Likes making models and three-dimensional figures (for example, LEGO structures).
IP	65. Forms friendships easily.
E	66. Questions the "fairness" of actions and incidents.

Adapted from the ideas of Howard Gardner. See his *Multiple Intelligences: New Horizons* (New York: Basic Books, 2006).

Sample Family Letter to Accompany "Multiple Intelligences Checklist"

Dear Family,

In order to help all my students succeed in school, I am gathering information about what each student knows and needs to learn. I am also asking students about the ways they prefer to learn. Some students, for example, like to learn by building and constructing, some prefer to read and discuss, and some learn best by drawing or sketching. By knowing more about how my students like to learn and about their strengths and interests, I can do a better job planning my curriculum.

You can help me get to know your child better. Included with this letter is a Multiple Intelligences Checklist. This checklist will give me information about how your child prefers to think and learn. It's based on the ideas of Dr. Howard Gardner of Harvard University. Gardner believes that all of us have thinking and learning strengths or preferences. In fact, he's described nine ways to think, learn, and show what we've learned. He calls these "multiple intelligences." People learn most easily in their areas of strength. However, Gardner also suggests that, with practice, we can improve our ability to use all nine ways of thinking.

Please read each item and put a checkmark beside any statement that you believe describes your child. There are no right or wrong answers. Please return the checklist to me by _____. Once I've read over your checklist, I will send you information about your child's preferred ways to learn.

Thank you!

Sample Family Letter to Report Results of "Multiple Intelligences Checklist"

Dear Family,

Thank you for completing the Multiple Intelligences Checklist. Based on your responses, I have checked the top three areas of preference for your child:

___ verbal/linguistic

___ logical/mathematical

___ visual/spatial

___ bodily/kinesthetic

___ musical

___ interpersonal

___ intrapersonal

___ naturalist

___ existential

This letter also includes two information sheets about what these preferences or "intelligences" mean. How We Think and Learn describes Howard Gardner's nine multiple intelligences, or ways of thinking. The second sheet, About Multiple Intelligences, lists important points to keep in mind about these thinking preferences and how students can use the information to help them do better in school.

The information from the Multiple Intelligences Checklist will help me in planning for your child at school. It may also help you as you work with your child at home. If you have any questions about multiple intelligences, feel free to call me at _____ or email me at _____.

Thank you for your help.

Verbal/Linguistic Intelligence
Multiple Intelligences Observations

List students' names on the numbered lines. Review the following list of verbal/linguistic characteristics with your students in mind. Go across each row, checking the characteristics that seem applicable to each student. (Or go down each column, considering each characteristic in turn.) Students with the highest number of checks exhibit verbal/linguistic strengths, based on your perceptions.

A. Loves to tell stories and engage in conversation and discussion.

B. Spells accurately and easily.

C. Is highly verbal and is able to clearly convey ideas orally.

D. Has a good memory for names, places, dates, and other facts.

E. Enjoys word games such as crossword puzzles, Scrabble, and acrostics.

F. Easily conveys thoughts and ideas in writing.

G. Has a good vocabulary in comparison to age peers.

H. Likes to read and do research to find out about topics of interest.

Student Names	A	B	C	D	E	F	G	H
1.								
2.								
3.								
4.								
5.								
6.								
7.								
8.								
9.								
10.								
11.								
12.								
13.								
14.								
15.								
16.								
17.								
18.								
19.								
20.								
21.								
22.								
23.								
24.								
25.								
26.								
27.								
28.								

Logical/Mathematical Intelligence
Multiple Intelligences Observations

List students' names on the numbered lines. Review the following list of logical/mathematical characteristics with your students in mind. Go across each row, checking the characteristics that seem applicable to each student. (Or go down each column, considering each characteristic in turn.) Students with the highest number of checks exhibit logical/mathematical strengths, based on your perceptions.

A. Is very interested in math.

B. Loves to chart, graph, map, and organize information.

C. Easily computes math problems mentally.

D. Enjoys working on logic puzzles or brainteasers.

E. Understands abstract ideas.

F. Is fascinated and challenged by computers; easily uses computers for more than playing simple games.

G. Usually prefers things to be orderly and logical.

H. Understands cause and effect, actions and consequences.

I. Is fascinated with numbers and statistics; has an excellent memory for such figures.

J. Enjoys chess, checkers, and other strategy games.

Student Names	A	B	C	D	E	F	G	H	I	J
1.										
2.										
3.										
4.										
5.										
6.										
7.										
8.										
9.										
10.										
11.										
12.										
13.										
14.										
15.										
16.										
17.										
18.										
19.										
20.										
21.										
22.										
23.										
24.										
25.										
26.										
27.										
28.										

Visual/Spatial Intelligence
Multiple Intelligences Observations

List students' names on the numbered lines. Review the following list of visual/spatial characteristics with your students in mind. Go across each row, checking the characteristics that seem applicable to each student. (Or go down each column, considering each characteristic in turn.) Students with the highest number of checks exhibit visual/spatial strengths, based on your perceptions.

A. Shows mechanical skill; can take things apart and put them back together easily.

B. Draws and sketches accurately and in detail.

C. Likes to sketch out ideas or represent them visually.

D. Learns best by seeing and observing; recalls information through images and pictures.

E. Enjoys puzzles, mazes, and other visual challenges.

F. Likes making models and three-dimensional figures.

Student Names	A	B	C	D	E	F
1.						
2.						
3.						
4.						
5.						
6.						
7.						
8.						
9.						
10.						
11.						
12.						
13.						
14.						
15.						
16.						
17.						
18.						
19.						
20.						
21.						
22.						
23.						
24.						
25.						
26.						
27.						
28.						

Bodily/Kinesthetic Intelligence
Multiple Intelligences Observations

List students' names on the numbered lines. Review the following list of bodily/kinesthetic characteristics with your students in mind. Go across each row, checking the characteristics that seem applicable to each student. (Or go down each column, considering each characteristic in turn.) Students with the highest number of checks exhibit bodily/ kinesthetic strengths, based on your perceptions.

A. Demonstrates balance, small- and large-motor dexterity, and precision in physical tasks.

B. Is well coordinated and has a good sense of timing.

C. Likes to move around and stay active.

D. Develops physical skills quickly and easily.

E. Enjoys acting things out, doing skits and plays; is dramatic.

F. Can mimic others' gestures or mannerisms.

G. Excels in sports or other physical activities.

H. Prefers to do things, rather than hear or read about them.

Student Names	A	B	C	D	E	F	G	H
1.								
2.								
3.								
4.								
5.								
6.								
7.								
8.								
9.								
10.								
11.								
12.								
13.								
14.								
15.								
16.								
17.								
18.								
19.								
20.								
21.								
22.								
23.								
24.								
25.								
26.								
27.								
28.								

Musical Intelligence
Multiple Intelligences Observations

List students' names on the numbered lines. Review the following list of musical characteristics with your students in mind. Go across each row, checking the characteristics that seem applicable to each student. (Or go down each column, considering each characteristic in turn.) Students with the highest number of checks exhibit musical strengths, based on your perceptions.

A. Remembers melodies.

B. Plays a musical instrument with ease and/or has a good singing voice.

C. Improvises vocal or instrumental music and/or composes music.

D. Shows a strong interest in music.

E. Shows a strong sense of rhythm in movement and speech.

F. Often sings or hums.

Student Names	A	B	C	D	E	F
1.						
2.						
3.						
4.						
5.						
6.						
7.						
8.						
9.						
10.						
11.						
12.						
13.						
14.						
15.						
16.						
17.						
18.						
19.						
20.						
21.						
22.						
23.						
24.						
25.						
26.						
27.						
28.						

Interpersonal Intelligence
Multiple Intelligences Observations

List students' names on the numbered lines. Review the following list of interpersonal characteristics with your students in mind. Go across each row, checking the characteristics that seem applicable to each student. (Or go down each column, considering each characteristic in turn.) Students with the highest number of checks exhibit interpersonal strengths, based on your perceptions.

A. Has leadership abilities; is able to influence others' opinions and actions.

B. Is sensitive to the feelings, thoughts, and motivations of others.

C. Prefers to work and learn with others.

D. Interacts comfortably and confidently with others.

E. Is able to organize and motivate others.

F. Forms friendships easily.

Student Names	A	B	C	D	E	F
1.						
2.						
3.						
4.						
5.						
6.						
7.						
8.						
9.						
10.						
11.						
12.						
13.						
14.						
15.						
16.						
17.						
18.						
19.						
20.						
21.						
22.						
23.						
24.						
25.						
26.						
27.						
28.						

Intrapersonal Intelligence
Multiple Intelligences Observations

List students' names on the numbered lines. Review the following list of intrapersonal characteristics with your students in mind. Go across each row, checking the characteristics that seem applicable to each student. (Or go down each column, considering each characteristic in turn.) Students with the highest number of checks exhibit intrapersonal strengths, based on your perceptions.

A. Asks questions about fairness; has a strong interest in right and wrong, justice and injustice.

B. Prefers to work independently; is self-directed.

C. Has a strong will.

D. Accurately identifies and conveys feelings.

E. Is comfortable with his or her individuality, regardless of peer pressure.

F. Has a strong sense of self.

G. Reflects on and ponders situations.

H. Recognizes and understands her or his personal strengths and limitations.

Student Names	A	B	C	D	E	F	G	H
1.								
2.								
3.								
4.								
5.								
6.								
7.								
8.								
9.								
10.								
11.								
12.								
13.								
14.								
15.								
16.								
17.								
18.								
19.								
20.								
21.								
22.								
23.								
24.								
25.								
26.								
27.								
28.								

Naturalist Intelligence

Multiple Intelligences Observations

List students' names on the numbered lines. Review the following list of naturalist characteristics with your students in mind. Go across each row, checking the characteristics that seem applicable to each student. (Or go down each column, considering each characteristic in turn.) Students with the highest number of checks exhibit naturalist strengths, based on your perceptions.

A. Is highly observant of surroundings.

B. Asks questions to seek more information about what he or she observes.

C. Is able to adapt and adjust to changing circumstances; is flexible.

D. Is "street smart"; understands how systems work and may use them to personal advantage.

E. Is interested in and sensitive to nature.

F. Can easily identify, categorize, and classify objects, information, and ideas.

Student Names	A	B	C	D	E	F
1.						
2.						
3.						
4.						
5.						
6.						
7.						
8.						
9.						
10.						
11.						
12.						
13.						
14.						
15.						
16.						
17.						
18.						
19.						
20.						
21.						
22.						
23.						
24.						
25.						
26.						
27.						
28.						

Existential Intelligence
Multiple Intelligences Observations

List students' names on the numbered lines. Review the following list of existential characteristics with your students in mind. Go across each row, checking the characteristics that seem applicable to each student. (Or go down each column, considering each characteristic in turn.) Students with the highest number of checks exhibit existential strengths, based on your perceptions.

A. Questions the "fairness" of actions and incidents.

B. Raises questions related to ethics or morals.

C. Is able to examine multiple points of view or perspectives.

D. Is able to compare and contrast opposing beliefs, viewpoints, or perspectives.

E. Exhibits a high level of care and concern for others.

F. Enthusiastically engages in service to others (fundraising, supporting issues of fairness and equity, volunteerism).

G. Enjoys examining philosophical and/or religious issues.

H. Exhibits high levels of concern for global, environmental issues.

Student Names	A	B	C	D	E	F	G	H
1.								
2.								
3.								
4.								
5.								
6.								
7.								
8.								
9.								
10.								
11.								
12.								
13.								
14.								
15.								
16.								
17.								
18.								
19.								
20.								
21.								
22.								
23.								
24.								
25.								
26.								
27.								
28.								

CHAPTER 3

What Do You Teach?

With the Common Core State Standards (CCSS),[1] your state or provincial content standards as well as additional learning goals possibly set by your school district, you've probably felt overwhelmed at times about what you must teach. Teachers' decisions about what's important for students to know, understand, and be able to do must be directed by the Common Core State Standards as well as required content standards of your state or province.

You may have reacted to the title of this chapter by thinking, I don't get to decide what to teach. Just remember that **while standards may direct your curriculum and focus your learning goals,** *how* **you teach to those standards—creative teaching—is still up to you.** If anything, standards-based education has encouraged teachers to ask themselves, "If this is where I have to take my students, how do I most effectively get them there?"

The most effective way to help students meet standards is by differentiating your instruction. The strategies of differentiated instruction can be used to modify and adjust any curriculum to respond to students' needs.

But standards aren't the only influence on your teaching decisions. Like most teachers, you're probably tempted by new topics and projects that appeal to your sense of fun and personal interests. Resource books, professional journals and magazines, materials displays at teacher conferences, and hundreds of lesson plan ideas on the Internet encourage us all to take side trips from the curriculum. And we all have favorite units we want to teach—even if they don't really fit curriculum goals. Given all the resources and all our ideas, how do we decide what's important to teach?

You may recall from Chapter 1 (page 5) that differentiated instruction is *relevant*, that is, it focuses on essential learning: those curricular objectives that are fundamental, significant, and most important for students to grasp. Appealing as a topic, a project, or an activity may be, unless it is firmly tied to your curriculum goals you need to set it aside.

Having gathered information about your students, it's time to look critically at what you want to teach them.

Essential Questions

Before planning differentiated activities, you must first identify the essential concepts and principles of your curriculum or subject based on Common Core State Standards and/or state or provincial content standards. Formulating "essential questions" will help you sort the crucial content from the fluff—the learning activities that take the focus away from *what is most important for students to know, understand, and do*.[2]

Essential questions go beyond factual information to uncover big ideas and significant learning. They identify overarching concepts or principles and reflect the big ideas of the established standards. **Essential questions reflect the key understanding you want your students to have after they've completed your curriculum.**

Why the question format? When learning goals are phrased as questions, they encourage inquiry rather than simply the production of facts and memorized responses.[3] The search for answers unifies a course or curriculum. Each unit, in turn, provides different perspectives on the questions.

---

[1] See *Aligning Your Curriculum to the Common Core State Standards* by Joseph T. Crawford (Thousand Oaks, CA: Corwin Press, 2011).

[2] For more on the importance of essential questions in differentiating instruction, see *Mapping the Big Picture* by Heidi Hayes Jacobs (Alexandria, VA: Association for Supervision and Curriculum Development, 1997) and *Understanding by Design* by Grant Wiggins and Jay McTighe (Alexandria, VA: Association for Supervision and Curriculum Development, 2005).

[3] Wiggins and McTighe (2005), p. 108.

Formulating essential questions for your curriculum will help you:

■ Identify the concepts or ideas that are most important for students to know and understand.

■ Focus your instructional planning.

■ Identify recurring themes that can unify a subject or curriculum across units.

Writing Essential Questions

To formulate essential questions for your curriculum, ask yourself:

■ What are the most important concepts in my course or subject area?

■ What is essential for my students to know and understand?

■ What concepts or ideas do we continue to refer to as we move through this curriculum?

Here are some tips for writing essential questions:[4]

■ Try to limit yourself to five questions. Too many questions can overwhelm you and your students. It is important to be realistic about the number of questions you can adequately address in the allotted time.

■ Identify key ideas, concepts, and/or themes. Specific content and skills will be addressed in your unit questions, see pages 55–56.

■ Make sure your questions reflect any required standards or learning goals.

■ Write questions in language you can share with students.

■ Avoid repetitious questions. Be sure each question focuses on a different concept or idea.

The following are examples of essential questions:

■ What characterizes leadership?

■ How are historical events influenced by physical and cultural geography?

■ How is the language of music (notes, meter, rests) represented on paper?

■ How does art reflect the time and the society it springs from?

■ What can we do to keep ourselves healthy and safe?

■ What characterizes great literature?

■ How do the systems of the human body work, and how do they work together?

■ How do authors' lives and experiences affect what they write?

■ How are number patterns used to represent mathematical relationships?

■ What effects do humans have on an ecosystem?

■ How do we collect and represent data?

■ How do matter, force, and energy interact?

■ How are mathematical patterns, relationships, and functions used to solve problems?

■ How are observation and theory used to study human interaction and development?

■ How do physical characteristics of animals reflect their habitats and life cycles?

■ How are the earth's features represented in geography?

Essential Questions as a Teaching Tool

Essential questions aren't just a planning and differentiation tool for teachers. They're a way to unify learning for students. No matter what grade you teach, your students will profit from seeing the connections among the various topics they're learning as well as the ways concepts discussed in one unit are revisited or broadened in a subsequent unit.

Here is an example of an essential question for sixth-grade social studies:

What characterizes leadership?

---

[4]Adapted from *Mapping the Big Picture* by Heidi Hayes Jacobs. Alexandria, VA: Association for Supervision and Curriculum Development. Copyright © 1997 ASCD. Reprinted by permission. All rights reserved.

The units might include:

- Exploration of the New World
- Colonization
- The Revolutionary War
- Westward Expansion
- The Civil War
- Reconstruction

Within each of these units, students explore various aspects of the essential question. For example:

Who were the leaders of this period of American history (for example, during the Civil War)?

What characteristics of leadership did each person possess (for example, Lincoln)?

As they return to the essential question in unit after unit, students discover what leadership entails through various periods of American history. To tie content from one unit to the next, you might ask students, for example, to explore the similarities and differences between Lincoln's leadership during the Civil War and Washington's leadership during the Revolutionary War. If your curriculum is organized around essential questions and if instruction flows from them, students should be able to answer essential questions from what they've learned in each unit.

Present your essential questions to students at the beginning of the year or your course. Allow time for questions and discussion; then post the questions on a bulletin board or classroom wall so you can refer back to them.

Unit Questions

Once you have developed essential questions, it's time to design unit-level questions. **Unit questions provide specific content and facts about essential questions. They add depth and specificity.**

Here are examples of essential questions followed by their associated unit questions:

Geography

Essential Question: What is geographical change?

Unit: Geography and climate of North America

Unit Questions:

1. What are the important seasonal and climatic changes in North America?
2. What natural forces have changed the geography of North America?
3. How has land use changed the geography of North America?
4. How have population changes in North America affected its geography?
5. How have people's use of land and water affected geography and climate in North America?

Life Science

Essential Questions:

1. What are living organisms?
2. What are some characteristics of living organisms?
3. How are living organisms classified in science?
4. What are common laws or principles of living organisms?
5. What are common cycles or patterns of living organisms?

Unit: Amphibians

Unit Questions:

1. What are the characteristics of amphibians?
2. What animals are included in the class *Amphibia?*
3. Which laws or principles of living organisms govern the life cycle of amphibians?
4. Which cycles or patterns of living organisms do amphibians follow?

Writing Unit Questions

Here are some tips for writing unit questions:

■ To distinguish between essential and unit questions, think BIG/little. Essential questions are the big ideas and concepts that you'll revisit throughout the year/course, even as you study different topics. Unit questions are subsets of essential questions that address specific content and skills.

■ Relate unit questions directly to essential questions to maintain your focus on what's important to teach.

■ Prioritize content by limiting the number of unit questions to five or fewer. Drop or set aside any content that takes you away from your questions.

■ Make the questions as interesting as possible, since, like your essential questions, you'll be sharing them with students.

■ Not every essential question will necessarily be addressed in each unit, nor will every essential question have only one unit question. It all depends on how the content flows in a particular unit.

Unit Questions as a Teaching Tool

As you begin each unit, post the unit questions with their corresponding essential questions. Refer back to both often so students can see the importance of the particular content you're presenting.

At the end of each unit, students should be able to answer each unit question—provided that you've based your curriculum on essential questions and your activities on unit questions. At the end of your course, students should be able to respond in detail to each essential question.

Using Essential and Unit Questions to Differentiate Instruction

Formulating essential questions and unit questions gives you a framework in which to differentiate activities. As you design activities that respond to students' needs, continue to ask

yourself: What learning experiences will enable my students to understand and answer my curriculum's essential questions? How can I vary my instruction so that more students can successfully answer my unit questions? Differentiated activities should be as relevant and significant as any other learning activity you ask your students to do. To determine the relevance of activities, examine how well they reflect essential and unit questions.

Choosing a Unit of Your Own

Use the form on page 69, Essential Questions and Unit Questions, to formulate questions for your course or curriculum, and for a specific unit. Here's the procedure for completing the form, as illustrated by the sample on page 63:

1. Subject. Select a subject you'd like to differentiate, such as algebra 1, third-grade reading, or American history. The sample subject is fourth-grade science.

2. Most important concepts. Consider: What are the most important concepts in this material that my students should investigate? What is essential for them to know and remember? List these on the form, indicating those concepts that address required Common Core State Standards and/or state or provincial content standards. Notice that on the sample two of the important concepts are related to curriculum standards: the interactions and interdependence of living systems and the interactions of people, places, and locations.

3. Essential questions. Write up to five essential questions that reflect these important concepts. Ask yourself: What concepts will I return to unit by unit throughout the year or during the course? Phrase your questions in language students will understand. For example: "What are some typical plants and animals that live in each biosphere?" Indicate questions that address content standards: for example, the sample question, "How do plants and animals interact in each biosphere?" relates to the content standard "the interactions and interdependence of living systems."

4. Unit/theme. Now choose one unit or theme you'd like to differentiate. Choose one that, from your experience, could be better presented with differentiated activities. A likely candidate is a unit or theme that includes learning goals that some students are close to mastering and some need more work on. If you're a beginning teacher or new to this grade level or course, simply select a unit you'd like to differentiate. This may be one you're particularly interested in or one you see as a special challenge. The sample unit is "Ocean Biosphere."

5. Unit questions. Write up to five unit questions that build on, elaborate on, and make more specific the essential questions you've formulated. Remember that unit questions convey specific facts and concepts in "student-friendly" language. For each unit question, identify the related essential question. In our example, the unit question "What are the characteristics of oceans?" relates to the first essential question, "What are the characteristics of a biosphere?"

Mapping Your Curriculum

When you filled out the Classroom Practices Inventory in Chapter 1 (pages 19–20), you saw how much you are already using the principles of differentiated instruction in your teaching. As mentioned, it's important to start where you are and to give yourself credit for what you're already doing.

Having formulated questions for a specific unit based on essential questions for your subject or curriculum, you're ready to examine that unit for its current level of differentiation. Then you can see where you might further differentiate, according to the particular needs in your classroom. An excellent tool for this examination is the curriculum map.

A curriculum map is an outline of a unit built from both essential questions and unit questions. **When you map your curriculum, you identify the content, skills, and products for a particular unit, as well as any Common Core State Standards and/or state or provincial content standards.** Such an outline shows you the foundations of a unit.[5]

F I G U R E   2

Essential Questions and Unit Questions: Sample

Subject: Fourth-grade science

Most important concepts (indicate those that address Common Core State Standards and/or state or provincial content standards)

- characteristics of biospheres
- plant and animal life of each biosphere
- interactions and interdependence of living systems *(content standard)*
- interactions of people, places, and locations *(content standard)*
- effects of humans on the biospheres

Essential questions (indicate those that address Common Core State Standards and/or state or provincial content standards)

1. What are the characteristics of a biosphere?
2. What are some typical plants and animals that live in each biosphere?
3. How do plants and animals interact in each biosphere? *(content standard)*
4. How does the geography of a biosphere affect human beings? *(content standard)*
5. How have human beings affected biospheres?

Unit/Theme: Ocean Biosphere

Unit questions (after each question, write the number of the related essential question)

1. What are the characteristics of oceans? (1)
2. What plants and animals live in oceans? (2)
3. What food chains link ocean plants with ocean animals? (3)
4. How does the geography of oceans affect human beings? (4)
5. How have human beings affected oceans? (5)

---

[5] Curriculum maps used in this book are based on concepts of mapping in *Mapping the Big Picture* by Heidi Hayes Jacobs. Alexandria, VA: Association for Supervision and Curriculum Development. Copyright © 1997 ASCD. Reprinted by permission. All rights reserved.

With an existing unit or one you've taught before, you may need to eliminate content, skills, or products that don't support your essential or unit questions. If you're developing a new unit, you'll map only those elements that address the core ideas you've formulated in your essential and unit questions. Reflecting on a unit in this way allows you to focus your planning on what will help students reach your curriculum goals.

Curriculum Maps: The How-To's

Photocopy the blank curriculum map on pages 70–71 and use it to map your unit. You'll be referring to this curriculum map at various points throughout the rest of this book. For example, you'll use it to make decisions about when, how, and under what circumstances you will differentiate instruction.

Figures 3 and 4 on pages 65 and 66 show examples of curriculum maps, one for fourth-grade science and one for tenth-grade geometry. Refer to them as you implement the following eight-point procedure for mapping your own curriculum:

1. Enter the subject or part of the curriculum under which this unit falls (fourth-grade science and tenth-grade geometry in the examples).

2. Write the theme or title of the unit you're mapping (Ocean Biosphere and Introduction to Geometry in the examples).

3. List the essential questions for your curriculum or subject (What are the characteristics of a biosphere? and What ways of thinking are used in mathematics? in the examples).

4. List the unit questions. After each, add the number of the related essential question (What are the characteristics of oceans? relates to the first essential question of fourth-grade science and What is geometric thinking? relates to the first essential question of tenth-grade geometry in the examples).

5. In the first column on the left, list any Common Core State Standards and/or content standards of your state or province.

6. In the second column, list content or topics covered in the unit, using general categories of information. For example, fourth-grade science students will study the geography of oceans. It's not necessary, however, to list all the geographic elements they'll cover (reefs, ocean shelf, and so on).

7. In the third column, list the skills you'll be focusing on in this unit. Include both critical and creative thinking skills as well as subject-specific skills and processes, such as hypothesis writing and interpreting data from charts and graphs. Texts, curriculum standards, and your school's curriculum guides often determine the skills you teach. For examples of skills frequently addressed in curriculum, see Figure 5, Sample Skills List, on page 67. (Geometry students in the example will learn to see objects geometrically, solve problems, and recognize invariants, among other skills.)

8. In the fourth column, list the projects or products you'll use to assess students' learning. How will students show or demonstrate what they've learned? Don't list daily activities, such as generating lists of ideas in a cooperative group or summarizing a reading. Instead, focus on tangible products or observable performances that require a greater commitment of student time or effort, or a more comprehensive demonstration of learning. (In the examples, fourth graders will develop a food chain web, compose a belief statement, and assemble a scrapbook. Tenth graders will use hand tools and software to make geometric constructions.) You can also list tests in this column; for example, tenth graders will take an end-of-unit test.

FIGURE 3

Curriculum Map: Sample

Subject: Fourth-grade science

Unit/Theme: Ocean Biosphere

Essential Questions	Unit Questions
1. What are the characteristics of a biosphere?	1. What are the characteristics of oceans?
2. What are some typical plants and animals that live in each biosphere?	2. What plants and animals live in oceans?
3. How do plants and animals interact in each biosphere?	3. What food chains link ocean plants with ocean animals?
4. How does the geography of a biosphere affect human beings?	4. How does the geography of oceans affect human beings?
5. How have human beings affected biospheres?	5. How have human beings affected oceans?

Asterisks (*) refer to exit points (see page 68) for differentiated activities.

Common Core State Standards and/or State or Provincial Content Standards	Content/Topics	Skills	Projects/Products
Common Core State Standards: Grade Four ***Informational Text*** • Integrate information from texts on the same topic in order to write or speak about the subject knowledgeably • Describe the overall structure (e.g., chronology, comparison, cause/effect, problem/solution) of events, ideas, concepts, or information in a text or part of a text ***Writing*** • Write opinion pieces on topics or texts supporting a point of view with reasons and information • Draw evidence from literary or informational text to support analysis, reflection, and research ***Speaking and Listening*** • Report on a topic or text, tell a story, or recount an experience in an organized manner using appropriate facts and relevant descriptive details to support main topics or themes, speak clearly at an understandable pace ***Social Studies/Geography Content Standard*** • Understand the interactions of people, places, and locations ***Science/Living Systems Content Standard*** • Understand the interactions and interdependence of living systems	Geography of oceans Ocean habitats Ocean animals Ocean plants Environmental issues/concerns	Identifying attributes* Determining cause/effect Classifying* Comparing/contrasting* Identifying relationships Inventing Problem solving Drawing conclusions Examining viewpoints	Scale drawing Food chain web Chart* Storytelling Illustration, mural, poster Venn diagram Belief statement Action plan* Lyrics Scrapbook Role play

Curriculum Map: Sample

Subject: Tenth-grade geometry

Unit/Theme: Introduction to Geometry

Essential Questions	Unit Questions

Essential Questions

1. What ways of thinking are used in mathematics?

2. How are mathematical thinkers problem solvers and problem posers?

3. What are essential tools for mathematics?

4. How is mathematical knowledge useful in everyday life?

Unit Questions

1. What is geometric thinking?

2. What is geometric problem solving?

3. How are algorithms used to describe shapes?

4. How do Escher-like figures represent geometric concepts?

Asterisks (*) refer to exit points (see page 68) for differentiated activities.

Common Core State Standards and/or State or Provincial Content Standards	Content/Topics	Skills	Projects/Products
Common Core State Standards: ***Mathematics/Geometry Congruence (G-CO)*** 1. Know precise definitions of angle, circle, perpendicular line, parallel line, and line segment, based on the undefined notions of point, line, distance along a line, and distance around a circular arc. 6. Given two figures, use the definition of congruence in terms of rigid motions to decide if they are congruent. 12. Make formal geometric constructions with a variety of tools and methods (compass and straight edge, string, reflective devices, paper folding, dynamic geometric software).	Standard geometric shapes Triangle inequality Geometric invariants Colinearity concurrence Congruence Bisectors Medians Continuous and discrete change	Seeing objects geometrically Geometric problem solving* Recognizing invariants: sum, product, ratio Proving theories from investigations Visualizing Analyzing Forming conjectures based on experiments Explaining and justifying conjectures Developing conjectures into proofs	Geometric constructions with a variety of tools including geometric software* Math journal* Portfolio of work samples Summative assessment

Sample Skills List

Following are examples of thinking and learning skills associated with analysis, critical thinking, and creative thinking.

Analytical Skills

identifying attributes

observing

discriminating same/different

comparing/contrasting

classifying

setting criteria

sequencing

identifying relationships

identifying patterns

predicting

determining cause/effect

comprehending analogies/metaphors

formulating

summarizing

making inferences

Critical Thinking Skills

analyzing trends

setting goals

making decisions

developing hypotheses

testing generalizations

inductive reasoning

deductive reasoning

distinguishing fantasy/reality

determining advantages/disadvantages

identifying point of view

determining bias

distinguishing fact/opinion

judging accuracy

determining relevance

judging credibility of sources

recognizing assumptions/fallacies

examining viewpoints

drawing conclusions

Creative Thinking Skills

fluency

flexibility

originality

elaboration

brainstorming

visualizing

inventing

finding problems

solving problems

Mapping Differentiation: Finding the "Exit Points"

Once your curriculum map is complete, you can examine your unit to see where it is already differentiated and where it would benefit from modification.

You'll note that on the sample curriculum maps, some entries are marked with an asterisk (*) to indicate potential "exit points" for differentiation. Exit points are times during the teaching of a unit when your curriculum diverges and various students "exit" the common instruction and activities because their learning needs differ from the core group. Some students may need more instruction and practice; others may be ready to move on. Some might benefit from a project that helps them apply what they've learned; others might benefit from a more challenging or in-depth activity. At exit points, you might also respond to students' learning *preferences* by offering a choice of projects. In short, **exit points yield differentiated activities.**

1. Start by examining the skills section of the map. From your experience, which of these seem likely to be harder for some students, easier for others? Which skills will require additional instruction, time, and practice for some students? Which could be extended for students who catch on easily? On the example map for fourth grade, the skills of identifying attributes, classifying, and comparing/contrasting have asterisks after them. This means that students will likely be at different points in their learning or have different learning needs. On the example map for tenth-grade geometry, the asterisk suggests that students will likely differ in their ability to solve geometric problems.

2. Next, review the list of projects and products. Some may be important for all students. Others might be differentiated: Are there times when some of your students could benefit from a more advanced or complex activity than what the rest of the class is doing? Are there times when you could give students a choice of project? These are also exit points, because students will work on different tasks based on their learning needs or preferences. Put an asterisk after projects that may be differentiated into basic and more advanced levels or into opportunities for student choice. For example, some fourth graders may do charts that share basic information; other students may do charts illustrating advanced, in-depth information. Some may share what they learned in a role play, others in a mural. Some tenth graders will be capable of more advanced geometric constructions or more complex approaches to the "Box Problem" than others.

Essential Questions and Unit Questions

Subject: _____

Most important concepts (indicate those that address Common Core State Standards and/or state or provincial content standards)

Essential questions (indicate those that address Common Core State Standards and/or state or provincial content standards)

1.

2.

3.

4.

5.

Unit/Theme: _____

Unit questions (after each question, write the number of the related essential question)

1.

2.

3.

4.

5.

Curriculum Map

Subject: _____

Unit/Theme: _____

Essential Questions

1.

2.

3.

4.

5.

(*) exit points

Common Core State Standards and/or State or Provincial Content Standards	Content/Topics

Unit Questions

1.

2.

3.

4.

5.

Skills	Projects/Products

PART 2

Differentiation in Action

CHAPTER 4

How Do You Teach?
Planning for Challenge and Variety

In Chapters 2 and 3, you gathered information about your students and examined your curriculum to determine what's essential to teach. On your curriculum map, you also identified potential places for differentiated activities by thinking about times when your students were typically in different places in their learning or could benefit from more advanced work. Now you are ready to find out how differentiated your current instructional plans are and to design, as appropriate, additional or alternative activities.

Many of you already have components and aspects of differentiated instruction in your plans. With some reflection on how you teach and how your students best learn, and with some careful review and revision of your instructional plans, you will be well on your way to a differentiated classroom.

Two familiar educational models, Bloom's taxonomy and Gardner's theory of multiple intelligences, can be applied to differentiation. In this chapter, you'll first review the different levels of thinking in Bloom's taxonomy, which can enable you to identify how challenging various learning activities are. Then you'll further explore the different ways of thinking and learning reflected in Gardner's model. You'll try out new ways to use the familiar.

This chapter describes how you can apply these two familiar models to your curriculum map in order to create a matrix plan for differentiated activities. Many teachers have found that the matrix formats make it quick and easy to use Bloom's and Gardner's models in their planning. Matrix plans can be an essential first step in differentiating instruction since they take what is and allow you to design what's missing. Matrix plans let you look systematically at your current instruction so you can more skillfully design differentiated learning activities that represent a spectrum of challenge and variety.

Challenge: Bloom's Levels of Thinking

Looking at instruction through **the lens of *challenge* means considering the rigor, relevance, and complexity of what you're teaching.** Learning that is challenging demands:

■ higher-level thinking that motivates all students to achieve.

■ substantive instruction that is clearly related to the essential curriculum.

■ content that has both depth and breadth.

Challenge does not mean simply more work, especially not more work of the same kind. Students rightfully resent being asked to take a challenge when it's clear to them that all it means is more work.

Educational psychologist Benjamin Bloom's *Taxonomy of Educational Objectives* (1956) presented a useful and time-tested model for examining and differentiating the challenge level of discussion questions and student tasks. In 2001, research by Lorin Anderson and David Krathwohl concluded a revision of the taxonomy. While all levels continue to accurately reflect student thinking and proved to continue to have value in designing both discussion questions and student tasks, there was one change in the taxonomy. In the original taxonomy, evaluation appeared at the highest level of thinking and synthesis as the second-highest level of challenge. Anderson and Krathwohl concluded that synthesis—innovative thinking—should be at the top of the taxonomy. They determined that the mental act of creativity (synthesis) is more complex than evaluation. In addition, the new taxonomy represents each level as an action verb indicating the cognitive process engaged in at each level: Recall (Knowledge), Understand (Comprehension), Apply (Application), Analyze (Analysis), Evaluate (Evaluation), and Create (Synthesis). All levels are of importance. The taxonomy's classifications can help you design student tasks that are appropriately rigorous, relevant to essential curriculum, and sufficiently complex. (See Figure 6.)

Students who are more academically talented will often need less time developing the solid base of facts, concepts, and ideas represented at the recall and understand levels of Bloom's model. At the same time, students who are less academically ready, or who generally require more time and practice to learn, also need to use higher-level thinking skills. We've all known students who had great difficulty remembering facts but were so creative they could easily function at the higher level of create. We've known others who would have given up in frustration and boredom if their tasks were too often limited to lower-level thinking. All students need opportunities to work at all levels.

Keep in mind that, by its very nature, **Bloom's higher levels of thinking reteach or reinforce basic content.** For example, when you ask students to identify the problem presented in a story and come up with an alternative solution, you're asking them to work at the level of analyze and evaluate. But to do this they need to revisit the story, recall what happened and recall the original solution. Thus you are reteaching the story through a more rigorous learning activity. Do all students need content knowledge? Absolutely. Do some students need more time than others to develop their content knowledge? Yes. Offering more time to students who need it while providing sufficient challenge for all is part of what differentiated instruction is about.

Bloom's taxonomy enables you to categorize activities by their level of challenge and complexity. You can then modify or adapt your activities—or even design new ones—to offer a wider range of thinking challenges and more opportunities for all students to use higher levels of thinking.

FIGURE   6

Bloom's Taxonomy*

Recall: The least complex kind of thinking asks students to recall facts and other information they have previously learned. When you ask students to tell, list, define, and label, you are eliciting this kind of thinking. *Example:* List China's most important exports.

Understand: The next level asks students to show their understanding of what they have learned. Directing students to explain, summarize, retell, or describe encourages them to think at the understand level. *Example:* Explain the reasons the Great Wall of China was built.

Apply: The apply level of thinking asks students to do something with what they have learned. When students demonstrate, construct, record, or use their knowledge, they are thinking at the apply level. *Example:* Organize a time line of the Ming Dynasty.

Analyze: When you ask students to take apart an idea and examine it critically, you are expecting analytical thinking. Activities like comparing and contrasting, classifying, critiquing, and categorizing call for analysis. *Example:* Compare and contrast the judicial systems of China and the United States.

Evaluate: Evaluate means determining the value or worth of something based on a set of criteria. Evaluation is usually preceded by analysis; in order to evaluate or judge something, students must look closely at (analyze) its characteristics or elements. When students judge, predict, verify, assess, or justify, they are thinking at the evaluate level of challenge. *Example:* Who do you think was the most influential figure in early Chinese history? Defend your choice.

Create: Create means putting things together in a new or different way, that is, inventing or reinventing, not simply reformatting. Creating requires creative thinking. Use care in distinguishing between apply and create levels. For example, an illustration involves *apply* thinking if the student simply uses or demonstrates factual knowledge, such as in a time line of historical events. Putting information into a new format (for example, from a textbook paragraph to a chart) is not create-level thinking since it does not require original thinking. An illustration involves the create level if it demands original thinking. Asking students to compose, hypothesize, design, and formulate encourages this challenging kind of thinking. *Example:* Compose a letter to the editor of a Chinese newspaper suggesting possible ways to resolve the conflict between the government and the people on personal rights and freedom.

---

*Based on *Taxonomy of Educational Objectives: Book 1 Cognitive Domain* by Benjamin S. Bloom, et al. (New York: Longman, 1984) and *A Taxonomy for Learning, Teaching, and Assessing: A Revision of Bloom's Taxonomy of Educational Objectives* edited by Lorin W. Anderson and David R. Krathwohl (Boston: Allyn & Bacon, 2000).

Using Bloom's Taxonomy to Differentiate Instruction

In differentiating instruction, a critical step is to ask, "How challenging is this learning activity?" To help you answer this question, Figure 7 (page 76) provides quick definitions of each of Bloom's levels, as well as verbs that you can use to develop and categorize activities at each level.

Variety: Gardner's Nine Ways of Thinking and Learning

The previous section examined your instruction through the lens of challenge and Bloom's levels of thinking: recall, understand, apply, analyze, evaluate, and create. This section looks at instruction through the lens of *variety*, that is, using different kinds of instructional strategies and products in your classroom.

As discussed in Chapter 2, Gardner's theory of multiple intelligences claims that **every student has strengths in thinking and learning**. (To review the nine intelligences, see How We Think and Learn, page 40.)

Students learn and produce with greater ease when they're using an area of strength. But keep in mind that multiple intelligences can be developed through practice. **Asking students to work in ways in which they're less able helps them strengthen those intelligences and widen their learning repertoire.** Not every concept must be taught in nine ways, nor do all

learning tasks and assessments need to match each student's thinking strengths. But **the more variety you offer students in the ways you ask them to learn and show what they have learned, the greater the likelihood of reaching more students.** (To review various products associated with Gardner's nine intelligences, see Projects, Presentations, Performances in Chapter 2, pages 34–38.)

How Differentiated Is Your Current Unit?

Let's start differentiating your current unit by examining how you're doing so far. By reviewing the curriculum map you started in Chapter 3, you can identify the level of challenge and variety already represented in your unit. It's easiest to start with "what is" and then do the necessary redesign or design work to better differentiate student activities.

Figure 8 on page 77 highlights the third and fourth columns in the sample curriculum map on ocean biosphere from Chapter 3 (page 65). Notice that each skill has been coded by its challenge level(s) in Bloom's taxonomy and each product has been coded by both its level(s) in Bloom and the Gardner intelligence(s) it represents. The key identifies each code.

As you can see in the Skills column, some skills require more than one thinking level just as some products call on more than one of Gardner's intelligences.

FIGURE 7

Challenge Levels

Level	Definition	Action	Activities
Create	Put together in a new or different way	Create It	compose, hypothesize, design, formulate, create, invent, develop, refine, produce, transform
Evaluate	Determine worth or value based on criteria	Judge It	judge, predict, verify, assess, justify, rate, prioritize, determine, decide, value, forecast, estimate
Analyze	Examine critically	Examine It	compare, contrast, classify, critique, solve, deduce, examine, differentiate, appraise, distinguish, experiment, question, investigate, categorize, infer
Apply	Use what you have learned	Use It	demonstrate, construct, record, use, diagram, revise, reformat, illustrate, interpret, dramatize, practice, organize, translate, manipulate, convert, adapt, research, calculate, operate, model, order, display, implement, sequence, integrate, incorporate
Understand	Show your understanding	Understand It	locate, explain, summarize, identify, describe, report, discuss, review, paraphrase, restate, retell, show, outline, rewrite
Recall	Recall facts and information	Know It	tell, list, define, label, recite, memorize, repeat, find, name, record, fill in, recall, relate

*Based on *Taxonomy of Educational Objectives: Book 1 Cognitive Domain* by Benjamin S. Bloom, et al. (New York: Longman, 1984) and *A Taxonomy for Learning, Teaching, and Assessing: A Revision of Bloom's Taxonomy of Educational Objectives* edited by Lorin W. Anderson and David R. Krathwohl (Boston: Allyn & Bacon, 2000).

F I G U R E   8

Curriculum Map: Sample

Subject: Fourth-grade science

Unit/Theme: Ocean biosphere

Curriculum Standards	Content/Topics	Skills	Projects/Products
Write and speak for a variety of academic purposes. *Inquiry* Gather information to answer questions. *Geography* Understand the interactions of people, places, and locations. *Living Systems* Understand the interactions and interdependence of living systems.	Geography of oceans Ocean habitats Ocean animals Ocean plants Environmental issues/concerns	Identifying attributes* **U, Ap, An, E** Determining cause/effect **An, E** Classifying* **An, E** Comparing/ Contrasting* **An, E** Identifying relationships **U, An, E** Inventing **An, C** Problem solving **An, E** Drawing conclusions **An, E, C** Examining viewpoints **An, E**	Scale drawing **Ap,** *LM, VS* Food chain web **U,** *VS* Chart* **U,** *VS* Storytelling **Ap,** *VL* Illustration, mural, poster **Ap,** *VS* Venn diagram **Ap, An, E,** *LM, VS* Belief statement **An, E, C,** *EX* Action plan* **An, E, C,** *VL* Lyrics **C,** *M* Scrapbook **U, Ap,** *VL, VS* Role play **Ap, An, C,** *VL, BK*

Key to Differentiated Activities *(*) exit points*

Bloom's Taxonomy

R = RECALL   U = UNDERSTAND   AP = APPLY   AN = ANALYZE   E = EVALUATE   C = CREATE

Gardner's Multiple Intelligences

VL = VERBAL/LINGUISTIC   LM = LOGICAL/MATHEMATICAL   VS = VISUAL/SPATIAL   BK = BODILY/KINESTHETIC

M = MUSICAL   Inter = INTERPERSONAL   Intra = INTRAPERSONAL   N = NATURALIST   EX = EXISTENTIAL

Coding Your Map for Differentiation

Now code your curriculum map (pages 70–71) so you can see how much challenge and variety is already in your unit:

1. On your map, review your list of skills. Using the key on page 77, code each skill by the relevant level(s) in Bloom's taxonomy. (To review the levels, see page 76.)

2. Next, review your projects and products column. Using the key, code each project/product using both Bloom's taxonomy *and* Gardner's categories. (To review the intelligences, see page 39.)

3. Review what you have:

■ What levels of the taxonomy are represented? What levels are missing? Pay special attention to the more challenging levels (analyze, evaluate, create). Do you have enough rigor and challenge?

■ Which multiple intelligences are well represented? Which are less well represented or missing? Do you have enough variety?

Adjusting Challenge and Variety

Now that you know the level of challenge and variety in your current unit, you may need to design or redesign some instructional activities that will either add greater variety or increase the challenge level of your activities.

This chapter presents a step-by-step method for designing differentiated activities combining content, process, and product. It also includes two matrix formats for planning differentiated units. Either of these planning formats—the matrix plan and the integration matrix—should enable you to organize your thinking and design differentiated units quickly. Many teachers tell me that the planning formats make differentiating instruction manageable. Try the one that appeals to you.

Writing Differentiated Activities: Short and Sweet

Analyzing, modifying, and designing learning activities will be easier if you phrase each learning description as succinctly as possible. The discipline of writing lessons in one, two, or three clear sentences encourages you to think about the components necessary for a challenging learning experience. Here's the formula:

content + process + product = the learning experience

content: What are students learning about?

process: What level of thinking is required?

product: How will the results of learning be represented and assessed?

The *content* of any activity reflects both essential and unit questions (as explained in Chapter 3, pages 59–63). *Process* reflects thinking processes and the level of challenge, as described in Bloom's taxonomy. The *product* is the end result of learning—how students show what they've learned. You can vary the products by using multiple intelligences to guide you as you design the activities.

Here's an example of a learning activity described in one sentence:

Compare and contrast a scene in a novel with the movie version of the same scene by presenting your ideas in a storyboard of words and pictures.

content = written and film versions of a scene from a novel

process = compare and contrast (analyze level of challenge)

product = storyboard of words and pictures (verbal/linguistic, visual/spatial product)

Sometimes you may need two or three sentences to clarify what students will learn and do. However, try to be as concise as possible.

Figure 9, page 79, shows other brief descriptions of learning activities. *Content* is italicized. Process words are underlined. **Products** are in boldface.

Appendix C (pages 159–160) presents an additional strategy that employs this technique for writing succinct lesson plans to create differentiated activities. Called the CCPP Toolkit (which stands for content catalysts, processes, products), this method offers a "menu" of processes and products that you can combine with content catalysts to actively engage your students in projects.

FIGURE 9

Brief Lesson Plans

Social Studies

■ Examine the issues surrounding the *use of the atomic bomb during World War II*. Establish your position, for or against, and compose a convincing argument to be presented in a **point/counter point dialogue.**

■ Gather and analyze *data showing the patterns of immigration in your community*. Present your results on a **bar graph.**

■ Compare and contrast *slavery in ancient Greece and Rome to slavery in the United States*. Present your information on a **display board.**

Language Arts

■ Write a **script** and role play a **scene** from a *fable.*

■ Use a **chart** to analyze the realistic and fanciful parts of a *science fiction story.*

■ Examine the conflicts between characters and within characters in a *novel*. Write an **essay** about your conclusions, *giving evidence* to support them.

Science

■ Predict the effects of *acids and bases* on various living and nonliving materials by conducting experiments and recording your conclusions in a **lab book.**

■ Construct a **map** of an *ecosystem* showing the interrelationships of plants, animals, and habitats.

■ Analyze how a particular change can be both beneficial and harmful to an organism's *habitat.* Create a **diagram** to show your conclusions.

Math

■ Applying your skills of *geometry*, create a **design** for a stained glass window.

■ Calculate the various *cookie ingredient combinations for several kinds of cookies* using butterscotch chips, chocolate chips, and walnuts, and using vanilla or chocolate cookie dough. **Chart** the possible combinations.

■ Build a **model** of a *miniature race car* and create a **scale drawing** that could allow others to build an accurate model.

Music

■ On a **chart,** categorize various *composers* according to musical style.

■ Compare *musical styles* by compiling an **audio recording** with music that shows each style.

■ Improvise an **interlude** in *vocal or instrumental music.*

The Matrix Plan

In addition to mapping your curriculum as described in Chapter 3 (see pages 63–68), the matrix offers another planning tool for curriculum units that specifically addresses levels of challenge. On your matrix, first categorize the instructional activities of a given unit according to the applicable thinking level(s) in the taxonomy. Sort each activity into the column that represents its Bloom's level. This step reveals how much challenge your unit activities offer. Then design or redesign activities as needed to better represent each thinking level or balance the activities across thinking levels.

The activities you plan on the matrix may be used with the whole class, small groups, partners, or individuals. Even if you go no further with differentiation than using a matrix plan as you design activities, you'll have taken an important step forward in increasing variety and challenge in learning activities and in reaching more students.

Take a look at the sample matrix plan on page 81. You'll see that learning activities for this unit have been written succinctly, noting content, the thinking processes students will use, and the product that will show their learning.

A Sample Matrix Plan

The following sample matrix, done for the ocean biosphere unit, shows three activities for each of the thinking levels. Depending on the number of activities you're planning for your unit, your matrix may not be completely filled in.

The number in parentheses following each activity indicates the order in which activities will be used. For example, the first activity in the unit is the recall-level activity of brainstorming animals and plants that live in the ocean. The second activity is the understand activity, in which students describe differences between lakes and oceans.

Keep in mind that students do not need to go through each level of Bloom's taxonomy in sequential order. The matrix lays out and codes the student activities for the entire unit on one sheet of paper. Once you've laid out the matrix, you are able to see whether a particular level of thinking is absent or underrepresented.

FIGURE 10

Matrix Plan: Sample

Unit/Theme: Ocean biosphere

Unit Questions: What are the characteristics of oceans? What plants and animals live in oceans? What food chains link ocean plants with ocean animals? How does the geography of oceans affect human beings? How have human beings affected oceans?

Bloom's Taxonomy

Recall	Understand	Apply	Analyze	Evaluate	Create
tell, list, define, label, recite, memorize, repeat, find, name, record, fill in, recall, relate	*locate, explain, summarize, identify, describe, report, discuss, review, paraphrase, restate, retell, show, outline, rewrite*	*demonstrate, construct, record, use, diagram, revise, reformat, illustrate, interpret, dramatize, practice, organize, translate, manipulate, convert, adapt, research, calculate, operate, model, order, display, implement, sequence, integrate, incorporate*	*compare, contrast, classify, critique, solve, deduce, examine, differentiate, appraise, distinguish, experiment, question, investigate, categorize, infer*	*judge, predict, verify, assess, justify, rate, prioritize, determine, decide, value, forecast, estimate*	*compose, hypothesize, design, formulate create, invent, develop, refine, produce, transform*
Brainstorm and list animals and plants that live in the ocean. (1)	Create a chart that shows the differences between an ocean and a lake in terms of smells, tastes, sounds, and appearance. (2)	In a collaborative group, illustrate the animals and plants that live at various depths of the ocean by designing a cut-paper mural. (6)		Identify the positives and negatives of living in either a coastal state or an inland state. Role-play a commercial convincing others to move to your state. (10)	Design a new ocean animal incorporating at least three characteristics of existing animals. Write a description of each characteristic, explaining your reasons for selecting it. (17)
In groups, research the migratory routes of gray, blue, right, or humpback whales, or of bottlenose dolphins. Locate and plot your animal's route on a world map, labeling its summer and winter habitats. (8)	Identify common characteristics of land and sea mammals. Explain the adaptations each kind of animal has made, based on habitat. Write a summary of your conclusions. (7)	Select a fable, myth, or tale of the sea. Present it to the class through storytelling. (11)	Examine the similarities and differences between land and sea geography. Present your comparisons in a Venn diagram. (3)	Collect and analyze articles from magazines and newspapers about current problems and issues related to ocean life. Create an ocean scrapbook and share it with the class. (12)	Create lyrics for a sea shanty or song about a sea adventure, or create a rap to teach facts about the sea. (13)
Using scale drawings, create life-sized drawings of at least five sea animals. Show and discuss size comparisons. (5)	In teams, research ocean plants and ocean animals. Make and arrange drawings to illustrate food chains. (4)	Create a poster or diagram showing high- and low-tide adaptations of a tidepool animal. (9)	Write a belief statement conveying your viewpoint and feelings about an environmental issue related to oceans, such as oil spills or offshore drilling. (16)	Collect data on threats to the habitats of at least three ocean animals. Determine trends and prioritize actions we must take to preserve ocean life. (15)	Develop an action plan to replace jobs in fishing communities lost due to fishing moratoriums. (14)

Based on a concept developed by Linda King and Barbara LeRose, Racine Public Schools, Racine, Wisconsin.

To recap, each of the columns deals with one thinking level in Bloom's taxonomy. The first cell lists the ways in which a student would display that level of thinking (under "Recall," a student would "tell, see, or find.") The next cell down the column describes an activity that reflects the relevant level of thinking (here, brainstorming a list of animals that live in the ocean). Finally, a number indicates the order in which the material typically would be presented. Note that each level of thinking offers different activities.

Differentiating Your Unit Using a Matrix Plan

A reproducible matrix plan appears on pages 86–87. Use it to differentiate activities for the unit on your curriculum map. Here's the procedure for planning on the matrix:

1. Consider the activities you've used for this unit or those suggested by the teacher's edition of your textbook. If you've taught the unit before, think about which activities were particularly worthwhile, successful, or engaging for your students. These might be your "keepers."

2. Write each "keeper" activity (or those from your teacher's edition that you consider worthwhile) in the content/process/product format (see pages 78–79). Referring as needed to the verbs listed on the matrix for each of the thinking levels, classify each activity by writing it in the appropriate box under its challenge level. For example, an activity asking students to compare/contrast, examine, or classify would be written in a box under the heading "Analyze."

You don't need to note such information as which pages you'll ask students to read. Nor should you classify activities that you yourself present. For example, if you draw a chart on the board and compare and contrast two animal phyla as a demonstration for your students, it is *you* who are at the analyze level, not your students. If your students construct the chart, then you would list that activity on the matrix plan. You only record what your students will *do*.

3. Now examine the overall level of challenge in the unit by seeing which of the levels of thinking are well represented and which are minimally addressed or missing.

4. Redesign or modify existing activities to balance the levels of challenge from low to high, or to increase the challenge level if you have too many lower-level activities. Remember that all students can think at all levels, depending on the task. Gifted and talented students find their most challenging activities at the analyze, evaluate, and create levels. Other students may need more practice with these levels of challenge in order to succeed.

5. You may wish to think about Gardner's multiple intelligences and examine the variety in your unit by reviewing the styles represented in the activities.

6. Now design new learning activities using levels of challenge that are missing or less well represented. Write your descriptions in the content/process/product format and include them on your matrix.

7. Once you've completed your activities, number them in the order you will use them with your students.

The Integration Matrix

If you want to use Bloom's challenge levels and Gardner's multiple intelligences together as you design your unit's activities, use the integration matrix on pages 88–89. This variation on the matrix plan includes Bloom's challenge levels across the top of the planning form and sample products categorized by Gardner's multiple intelligences down the side.

To use the integration matrix:

1. Think about new or current activities you wish to use with this unit. Think about the Bloom's level of each activity as well as the Gardner product it represents. (For example, summarizing the plot of a book by constructing a time line of events in the story is an understand level activity using logical/mathematical products.)

2. Place each activity in the box below its appropriate Bloom's label and across from its designated Gardner grouping. (The sample time line activity would be placed in the matrix box below the understand level and across from logical/mathematical.)

3. Review the activities you have categorized and determine whether any activities need to be redesigned or new ones developed so that your unit represents a balance of higher-order thinking and a variety of products.

The integration matrix enables you to use both Bloom's and Gardner's models simultaneously. When you do so, you develop particularly strong and well-differentiated activities.

Figure 11, pages 84–85, shows a sample integration matrix for secondary-level students. As on the matrix plan, the numbers indicate the sequence of activities in the unit. Several activities with the same number (such as 8 on the sample integration matrix) indicate that students are being given a choice of activities to complete. Items with a number and a letter (for example, 4a, 4b, 4c) indicate multiple steps in an activity represented in different areas of the matrix.

FIGURE 11

Integration Matrix: Sample

Unit/Theme: Twentieth-century American novel

Unit Questions: How does a novel reflect its times and the novelist's personal history? How are characters developed in a novel? How are symbols used to convey meaning in a novel?

Bloom's Taxonomy	Recall	Understand	Apply	Analyze	Evaluate	Create
	tell, list, define, label, recite, memorize, repeat, find, name, record, fill in, recall, relate	locate, explain, summarize, identify, describe, report, discuss, review, paraphrase, restate, retell, show, outline, rewrite	demonstrate, construct, record, use, diagram, revise, reformat, illustrate, interpret, dramatize, practice, organize, translate, manipulate, convert, adapt, research, calculate, operate, model, order, display, implement, sequence, integrate, incorporate	compare, contrast, classify, critique, solve, deduce, examine, differentiate, appraise, distinguish, experiment, question, investigate, categorize, infer	judge, predict, verify, assess, justify, rate, prioritize, determine, decide, value, forecast, estimate	compose, hypothesize, design, formulate, create, invent, develop, refine, produce, transform
Gardner's Multiple Intelligences						
Verbal/Linguistic poetry, debate, storytelling, essay, checklist, journal	As you read your novel, record at least five phrases, word choices, sections of dialogue, or descriptions that you found interesting. Share your selections and reasons for selecting each with a partner reading the same novel. (1)	Identify the historical context of your novel. What was taking place socially, economically, and politically at the time of its publication? Write an information brief as if you were a journalist of the time. (5a)	Research the life of your author, including background, upbringing, life experiences, and personality. Write a short descriptive piece that could serve as an introduction to a review of your novel. (4a)	Select one main character to analyze in a character journal. For each chapter: 1. List 2-3 key quotations from or about the character. 2. Examine the character's actions, behavior, and reactions. 3. Select one word that best represents the character. (7)		
Visual/Spatial drawing, model, poster, photograph, storyboard, illustration, board game		Describe your novel's characters and their relationships to each other by creating a relationship map. (2)			Develop a visual or musical representation of your main character. Include physical characteristics, personal attributes, and change and/or growth as represented in the novel. (8)	Assess the use of symbols in your novel, looking at characters, dialogue, actions and interactions, and physical objects. On an illustrated poster, show each symbol and give your interpretation of its meaning. (11)
Logical/Mathematical diagram, outline, timeline, chart, critique, graph		Summarize the plot of your book by constructing a timeline of events, chapter by chapter. (3)		Diagram how your novel represents its social, economic, and political times. Include, as appropriate, characters, setting, plot, points of view. (5b)		Determine how your author's life or experiences may have influenced or been represented in the novel. Chart any similarities. (4b)

Intelligence	Descriptors	Activity
Naturalist	classification, collection, solution to problem, display, observation, forecast, investigation, simulation, exhibit, identification	If your main character lived today, what kinds of things would you find in his/her backpack, briefcase, duffel bag, or purse? Collect and organize items to display to the class. Be ready to defend your selections with evidence from the novel. (9)
Musical	song, rap, lyrics, composition, jingle/slogan, melody	Develop a visual or musical representation of your main character. Include physical characteristics, personal attributes, and change and/or growth as represented in the novel. (8)
Bodily/Kinesthetic	role play, skit, pantomime, dance, invention, lab, improvisation, prototype	Taking the role of your novel's narrator, dramatize a scene or an action sequence. Audio or video record your dramatization. (6)
Intrapersonal	journal, log, goal statement, belief statement, self-assessment, editorial	Is there a message, lesson, or reflection in your novel that is applicable to your life or circumstances? In your journal, write about what you've learned through reading and reflecting on this novel. (10)
Interpersonal	discussion, roundtable, service learning, conversation, group activity, position statement, interview	With students who read other novels, discuss similarities and differences in novels and in authors' lives. (4c)
Existential	exploring theories and ideas, solving moral dilemmas, considering the fairness of an issue, examining personal beliefs and viewpoints, comparing and contrasting beliefs and viewpoints, considering the effects on the environment and on others, studying philosophy or religions, helping other people	Consider a dilemma that was presented to a character in the novel. Formulate an alternative plan of action considering the effects on other characters or the storyline. Present your ideas in an essay or a graphic-novel story strip. (12)

Matrix Plan

Unit/Theme: _____

Unit Questions:

1._____

2._____

Bloom's Taxonomy

Recall	Understand	Apply
tell, list, define, label, recite, memorize, repeat, find, name, record, fill in, recall, relate	*locate, explain, summarize, identify, describe, report, discuss, review, paraphrase, restate, retell, show, outline, rewrite*	*demonstrate, construct, record, use, diagram, revise, reformat, illustrate, interpret, dramatize, practice, organize, translate, manipulate, convert, adapt, research, calculate, operate, model, order, display, implement, sequence, integrate, incorporate*

Based on a concept developed by Linda King and Barbara LeRose, Racine Public Schools, Racine, Wisconsin.

3._____

4._____

5._____

6._____

7._____

Analyze	Evaluate	Create
compare, contrast, classify, critique, solve, deduce, examine, differentiate, appraise, distinguish, experiment, question, investigate, categorize, infer	*judge, predict, verify, assess, justify, rate, prioritize, determine, decide, value, forecast, estimate*	*compose, hypothesize, design, formulate, create, invent, develop, refine, produce, transform*

Integration Matrix

Unit/Theme: _____

Unit Questions:

Bloom's Taxonomy	Recall	Understand	Apply	Analyze	Evaluate	Create
	tell, list, define, label, recite, memorize, repeat, find, name, record, fill in, recall, relate	*locate, explain, summarize, identify, describe, report, discuss, review, paraphrase, restate, retell, show, outline, rewrite*	*demonstrate, construct, record, use, diagram, revise, reformat, illustrate, interpret, dramatize, practice, organize, translate, manipulate, convert, adapt, research, calculate, operate, model, order, display, implement, sequence, integrate, incorporate*	*compare, contrast, classify, critique, solve, deduce, examine, differentiate, appraise, distinguish, experiment, question, investigate, categorize, infer*	*judge, predict, verify, assess, justify, rate, prioritize, determine, decide, value, forecast, estimate*	*compose, hypothesize, design, formulate, create, invent, develop, refine, produce, transform*
Gardner's Multiple Intelligences						
Verbal/Linguistic poetry, debate, storytelling, essay, checklist, journal						
Visual/Spatial drawing, model, poster, photograph, storyboard, illustration, board game						
Logical/Mathematical diagram, outline, timeline, chart, critique, graph						

Naturalist classification, collection, solution to problem, display, observation, forecast, investigation, simulation, exhibit, identification	*Musical* song, rap, lyrics, composition, jingle/slogan, melody	*Bodily/Kinesthetic* role play, skit, pantomime, dance, invention, lab, improvisation, prototype	*Intrapersonal* journal, log, goal statement, belief statement, self-assessment, editorial	*Interpersonal* discussion, roundtable, service learning, conversation, group activity, position statement, interview	*Existential* exploring theories and ideas, solving moral dilemmas, considering the fairness of an issue, examining personal beliefs and viewpoints, comparing and contrasting beliefs and viewpoints, considering the effects on the environment and on others, studying philosophy or religions, helping other people

Many Uses for Your Matrix

Your matrix can serve as a differentiation "insurance policy." By using either planning format, you'll be assured that each differentiated unit reflects various levels of challenge, with an emphasis on higher-order thinking. You'll also feel confident that you've reached more students by providing greater variety in the ways they learn and represent their learning.

Either planning format, the matrix plan or integration matrix, can help you in other ways as you differentiate instruction. Use them to:

■ Provide a slate of activities to select from as you build a unit.

■ Plan activities to be used with all students in your classroom.

■ Design tiered activities for flexible instructional groups (see Chapter 6, pages 97–106).

■ Develop "project menus" that offer students a choice (see Chapter 7, pages 111–113).

■ Design challenging questions (see Appendix B, pages 151–158).

CHAPTER 5

What Do Students Need?
Flexible Instructional Grouping

Now that you have looked at your curriculum and learning activities in terms of challenge and variety, you may be asking: How do I arrange my classroom to accommodate students with different learning needs? What does differentiated instruction actually look like in a classroom from day to day?

Take a moment to review the classroom examples in Chapter 1 (pages 5–6). You'll see that the most important characteristic distinguishing the classrooms of Larry Kimmer and Marie Fuentes was their use of grouping. Without calling attention to which students were working together, Larry and Marie put together small groups with similar learning needs. At other times— perhaps using information collected from Projects, Presentations, Performances, on pages 34–38, they might group students according to their learning preferences. Or they might use the index cards generated from the Interest Inventory, on pages 29–31, to create cooperative learning groups. This **flexible use of student groups is the heart of differentiated instruction.**

Like most teachers, you probably have students work in small groups at times, usually for particular activities or projects. Depending on the task, you may arrange groups yourself or let students choose with whom they work. Your groups may sometimes be heterogeneous and sometimes arranged according to students' aptitude or ability. Flexible instructional grouping, however, is specifically intended to provide a better instructional match between students and their individual needs. **When you group flexibly, you create instructional groups and prescribe specific activities that respond to students' learning needs.**

Personalizing Learning with Flexible Grouping

Flexible instructional grouping is a critical management strategy in a differentiated classroom. It lets you personalize learning activities according to students' needs, and, in the process, gives you time to provide additional instruction or extended learning experiences to particular students or groups. Flexible grouping does this without taking away from a classroom's sense of community. You'll find, in fact, that students feel more involved, engaged, and confident when they're involved in activities tailored to their learning needs and preferences. Your instructional time is better used because you're able to address appropriate learning goals for all students.

Flexible grouping is not used daily, but as needed. It does not create permanent groups; needs and circumstances determine who students work with. Group size varies, depending on the number of students with similar learning needs. The group's activity time varies according to the complexity of the task. Groups may work together for one day or several, for one class period or several, and they may work at different times and different days of the week.

Flexible Grouping at Exit Points

The optimum times for flexible grouping are at the exit points you noted on your curriculum map (pages 70–71). This might happen at two points: (1) When some students haven't yet mastered skills or content and others are ready to move on, or (2) when some students would benefit from an advanced task and others from a more basic activity. These are exit points in which you group students according to common instructional needs. For example:

■ **Progress on the learning continuum.**Which students need more time, practice, or instruction? Which students are ready to move on or ready to pursue activities that extend their learning? In other words, which students are at a foundational level with this particular content or skill and which have advanced beyond the foundations?

■ **Learning preferences or strengths.** Which students have bodily/kinesthetic learning strengths? Which are strong in intrapersonal thinking and doing? Which prefer verbal/linguistic learning? Are they auditory, visual, or kinesthetic learners. How do individual students prefer to show what they've learned?

Flexible Grouping Compared with Other Grouping Strategies

Flexible grouping is just one of several techniques for responding to learner differences. Let's take a look at the differences between flexible grouping and four other ways of grouping students.

Tracking: Students are grouped according to general learning abilities, rather than particular talents or limitations, for example, in math or language arts. Groups stay together for all or most subjects every day and students rarely move out of their groups—even from year to year.

Ability or aptitude grouping: Students are grouped according to scores on standardized tests of aptitude, intelligence, or ability. If the groups stay together for all or most subjects, this grouping method becomes tracking.

Performance grouping: Students are grouped according to grades or performance in a particular subject area—for example, accelerated, enriched, or advanced placement classes.

Cooperative grouping: Students are grouped for collaborative work, either by the teacher or by student choice.

Flexible instructional grouping: Students are grouped according to their learning needs, strengths, and preferences. Grouping is changed regularly to match student needs to the task at hand.

It is particularly important to understand the distinctions among ability/aptitude groups, cooperative groups, and flexible groups. (See the chart on page 93.) Keep in mind, though, that even in a class of students grouped by aptitude or performance, you can still use flexible grouping techniques to good advantage. You'll have a narrower range of abilities and learning differences than in a heterogeneous class, but you'll still see variations in learning pace, preferences, and interests that are best addressed by flexible grouping.

FIGURE 12

Three Kinds of Groups

Flexible Groups	Ability/Aptitude Groups	Cooperative Groups
Determined by teacher perceptions or evidence of learning needs.	Determined largely by scores on standardized tests of intelligence or aptitude.	Determined by the teacher or student choice.
Based on specific learning needs, strengths, or preferences.	Based on general performance or achievement.	Usually random as to student ability or learning preferences.
Fluid group membership.	Rigid group membership.	Fluid group membership.
Groups work on different activities based on needs, strengths, or preferences.	Groups all tend to work on the same or similar activities.	Each group works on the same task or on one facet of the same task.
Students are grouped and regrouped as appropriate for particular activities.	Students may or may not be regrouped within the classroom based on instructional needs.	Students may be purposely mixed as to learning needs and academic strengths to provide peer instruction or leadership within groups.
Occurs as needed.	Occurs daily.	Occurs when a task seems appropriate.
Grouping based on individual students' skill proficiency, content mastery, learning preferences or interests.	Grouping based on perceptions about innate ability.	Grouping for the purpose of developing collaborative skills.

Questions and Answers About Flexible Grouping

Are flexible groups suitable for cooperative learning?

Yes. The activities you assign to students within a flexible group may be done cooperatively or collaboratively—they may also be done with a partner or as an individual assignment. **All students in a flexible group are doing the same activity, but whether the task is done individually or with others is up to you.**

If I use flexible instructional grouping, does that mean I don't use whole-group instruction anymore?

Flexible grouping is a key technique of differentiated instruction, but differentiating doesn't mean you no longer teach the whole class at once. **Sometimes whole-group instruction is your most effective teaching method.** For example, you'll want to instruct the whole class when you're:

■ building community through common activities or experiences.

■ introducing new units, topics, skills, or concepts.

■ conducting discussions of important content.

How often should I use flexible groups?

You form flexible groups as needed. As mentioned, the most important times to use this strategy are at exit points in your curriculum, when students' learning needs vary significantly. Form flexible groups when some students need more time and instruction or a basic application activity and others need a more advanced activity or new content. In order to break the pattern for students who tend to be placed in either reteaching or advanced groups, form groups based on interests or learning preferences from time to time.

Does flexible grouping take the place of accelerated, enriched, or advanced placement classes?

No. Such classes are important ways to provide advanced learning opportunities to students who need them. Students are grouped by common instructional needs, as in flexible groups. However, unlike the changing composition of flexible groups, students in these classes meet on a regular basis. As mentioned earlier in connection with ability grouping, advanced students will still benefit from flexible grouping.

If I usually use flexible grouping to respond to students' learning needs, doesn't that mean that some students will always be doing advanced work while others will always be doing basic or reteaching activities?

We've noted the importance of making differentiation invisible to students to avoid hurt feelings or resentment. **The key to making differentiation invisible is varying your instructional strategies.** Sometimes students learn together as a class; other times they work in groups, with a partner, or independently. Sometimes they select their own group, partner, or task; sometimes you select for them. You use flexible groups to meet learning needs, but you're careful to group students by interests and learning preferences at other times. For example, if a student is usually placed in a reteaching group but knows a lot about popular music, you might place her in a cooperative group with students of varying academic abilities for a project on musical genres. If another student struggles with language but is a talented artist, you might group him with other artistic students for a particular project. "Flexible" means just that—you mix things up whenever possible to meet specific needs, including the need for a sense of community in your classroom. (More will be said about invisibility when we look at tiered assignments on pages 104–106.)

Tips on Managing Flexible Groups

When you're just beginning to differentiate instruction, it may seem overwhelming to think of managing multiple learning tasks simultaneously in your classroom—particularly if you've relied on whole-group instruction or have mainly formed cooperative groups in which students do the same task. You need to decide how to move students into the appropriate learning task; how to provide instructions, clarification, and support; and how to give yourself adequate time with each group.

Even teachers who have done flexible grouping for some time, and whose students are used to this way of learning, can be caught by the unforeseen. Here are some ideas to help you think through and plan what you want students to do and how you want them to do it:

1. If students are to do an activity collaboratively, consider dividing a larger instructional group into smaller teams of four or five. Smaller groups can be easier to manage and more effective for learning, since students have a greater opportunity to contribute.

2. Be flexible about how much time you spend with each group. Don't feel you need to spend the same amount of time with each. Allocate time based on a group's need for direct instruction and teacher feedback.

3. As necessary, allow yourself more time with groups you suspect will require additional attention by planning activities for other groups who need only minimal direction.

4. Create tasks that students can manage by themselves after you give directions. Provide a checklist of procedures or steps for students to follow as they complete an activity.

5. Provide checklists or rubrics to convey your expectations about the quality of students' work. As appropriate, provide samples or examples to guide them.

6. Establish behavior guidelines for flexible group time. How much noise is appropriate for today's activities? Teach students the difference between productive and disruptive noise. Who are students to talk to and work with? How much freedom do they have to move about the classroom? Where in the room can each group work most productively? How are they to get and return any materials they need?

7. Provide guidance for when and how students can get assistance from you. Establish a method for letting them know when you're free to answer questions or provide feedback.

8. Convey your expectations about students' individual accountability for using time effectively. What evidence is needed to show their accomplishments during a class period? If an activity is to take more than one period or day, will they have a work-in-progress folder that you can review?

9. Establish procedures for what to do when students are finished. Where should they put their completed work? What do they do if they finish early? What about work that's still unfinished at the end of class?

10. To bring everyone together, consider a whole-group activity, reflection, or sharing of work at the beginning or end of class time. Providing opportunities for all students to share what they're doing shows that you value everyone's work.

Flexible Grouping Across Classrooms

Many teachers find that forming flexible groups with another teacher and class solves many management problems. For example, Jack Evans and Estelle Carter are moving through their fifth-grade math curriculum at a fairly even pace.

During lunch on Monday, they discuss their students' progress in division. Both have students who need further instruction and practice and others who are ready for more advanced work. They decide they'll group for instruction on Wednesday. Jack will plan a lesson for students in both classes who need more instruction and practice. Estelle will plan an extension or enrichment lesson for students who are ready to move on. On Wednesday, both teachers present a list of students assigned to each of the classrooms. Students moving to the other classroom gather the materials they need and take their seats in the other room. Next time they flexibly group, Estelle and Jack rotate their roles: she may take the reteaching group and he may take the advanced learners.

Student Independence and Flexible Groups

Some students have had little experience with small groups doing different activities. Some may have difficulty adjusting to higher levels of responsibility and independence. In planning for flexible instructional grouping, you need to think about the learners in your classroom. They will vary in the amount of direction and degree of structure they need in order to learn and perform successfully in groups. If you are aware of and plan for such differences, your flexible grouping will run more smoothly. Keep these thoughts in mind as you plan:*

1. All students need new content and skills presented to them. It may be most effective for you to provide this through whole-group instruction.

2. Students who learn quickly and easily tend to need less information about how to go about their work and less teacher feedback about their progress. Provide clear directions and then expect them to get to work.

3. Some students need more direction about what to do and how to do it. They need specific,

easy-to-understand directions and precise procedures for completing an activity. Provide a checklist of procedures, or if you have time, put the directions on an audio recording that they can replay as needed.

4. Students with a strong preference for working independently may resist being placed in groups. You may want to offer these students the option of working independently or choosing a partner from within the flexible group.

5. Some students and some age groups need more supervision than others. Some may have a difficult time staying with an activity unless you're there to encourage them. Structure your activities so these students are very clear about what to do and when to do it. Organize your time so you can provide clarification, encouragement, and feedback.

6. Some students love to socialize and may be easily sidetracked into conversations that are unrelated to the task at hand. Set up clear behavior guidelines so they'll know if and when they can talk with others and what they should be talking about.

Now that you've explored flexible grouping and the different ways you can arrange your classroom to accommodate different learning needs, the next question is: How do you tailor activities to your flexible groups? The answer is tiered assignments. Tiered assignments are the instructional components of flexible grouping and the subject of the next chapter.

---

*As suggested by Thomas L. Good and Jere E. Brophy in *Looking in Classrooms* (Boston: Allyn & Bacon, 2007).

CHAPTER 6

What Do Students Need?

Tiered Assignments

Tiered assignments are differentiated learning tasks and projects that you develop based on your diagnosis of students' needs. When you use tiered assignments with flexible instructional groups, you are prescribing particular assignments to particular groups of students. Within each group, you decide whether students do the task alone, with a partner, or as a collaborative learning team.

Just as flexible instructional groups differ from other kinds of groups, tiered assignments differ from other group assignments. Like flexible groups, **tiered assignments are intended to provide a better instructional match between students and their individual needs**. While teachers have typically used group assignments to promote collaborative or cooperative skills, tiered assignments are based on students' common learning needs.

As you design tiered activities, it's important to refer to your curriculum map. For tiered assignments to be relevant, significant learning, they must add depth and breadth to students' understanding of essential questions and unit questions.

Six Ways to Structure Tiered Assignments

Tiering can be based on challenge level, complexity, resources, outcome, process, or product. You determine the best approach based on the specific learning need you're addressing. See pages 101–102 for guidelines.

Tiered by Challenge Level

You can use Bloom's taxonomy as a guide to developing tasks at various levels of challenge. For example, here are elementary-level activities tiered by challenge level for a unit on amphibians:

Apply level: After reviewing the information about frogs and toads from the Department of Natural Resources, record the characteristics of each on a chart.

Analyze level: After reviewing the information about frogs and toads from the Department of Natural Resources, create a Venn diagram comparing and contrasting these two amphibians.

The apply activity asks students to pull information from a source other than their textbook and use it in a chart. The activity is a reteaching opportunity, because it allows students who have not yet mastered the content to revisit it through a new resource. The analyze activity is for students who have already demonstrated mastery of basic content. Since these students will benefit from a more challenging activity, they're asked to analyze information from the new resource and to diagram comparisons.

Here's an example of activities tiered by challenge level for a middle school or high school unit on advertising and propaganda:

Apply level: Review the ads in a teen magazine. Identify each by propaganda technique (such as bandwagon, testimonial, or slogan) and make a collage or poster illustrating the techniques you find.

Analyze/Evaluate level: Review the ads in a teen magazine. Examine the characteristics of the "ideal" teen girl and guy portrayed in the ads. Create a collage or poster to share your conclusions about advertising's portrayal of "ideal" teens.

The apply-level activity would be most appropriate for students who need reinforcement of content or more practice at recognizing propaganda methods. Students are asked to apply what they know in making the collage or poster. The analyze/evaluate activity would be best for students who already have a firm understanding of propaganda methods. They're asked to extend what they know about propaganda to the messages projected by advertising and to draw some conclusions about the use of images in ads. Since both activities involve reviewing ads in a teen magazine, students would probably find them fair and equally interesting. Both groups are asked to share the results of their work and thus contribute to the learning of the whole class. Students might also get the opportunity to discuss the collages or posters. It's critical to the success and acceptance of tiered assignments that everyone's work is honored.

Tiered by Complexity

When you tier activities by complexity, you address the needs of students who are at introductory levels of learning as well as those who are ready for more abstract, analytical, in-depth, or advanced work. Be sure that the tasks you design are truly more advanced and not simply more work. When one group of science students is asked to use two references for research and another group is asked to use five references for research, the second group isn't doing a more advanced task—they are doing the same task but with more work. (This is covered in more detail in Making Tiering Invisible, pages 104–106.)

Here are three sample activities tiered by complexity:

Least complex: Create an informational brochure that will inform your classmates about an environmental issue related to rainforests.

More complex: Create an informational brochure that will inform your classmates of different points of view about an environmental issue related to rainforests.

Most complex: Create an informational brochure that presents various positions on an environmental issue related to rainforests. Determine your position on the issue and present a convincing argument for it in your brochure.

In these examples, all students are asked to research a topic and to design an informational brochure, but the focus of their research differs. Brochure content varies from factual to analytical to persuasive. Presentation of research ranges from fairly simple to complex.

The following activity, tiered by complexity, was developed by middle school math teachers for use with flexible instructional groups at the beginning of the school year. Students were assigned to the task best suited to their learning needs.*

Tiered Activity

Teacher directions:

Students are divided into groups of 4 to 6. Each group works with the same story but is given one of two lists of data: the groups comprising Team 1 get data for a more basic activity, while the groups comprising Team 2 get data for a more advanced activity. Each group is to create a 5- to 10-minute skit based on their story and data. The skit is to include the math Susie uses to calculate how much money she has left.

Here's the story . . .

Susie starts her evening with $22.18. She wants to keep track of how much she spends. First, she and her three friends go to the school dance. After the dance, they go out for pizza. On their way home, they pass by a music store. Susie heard some new music at the dance and now decides to buy the CD. How much money does Susie have left when she gets home?

Team 1	Team 2
Here's the data . . .	**Here's the data . . .**
7% sales tax	6.5% sales tax
Dance ticket: $2.50	Dance ticket: $2.50
Pizza Place Pitcher of pop: $2.99 Pizza: $6.99	Pizza Place Pitcher of pop: $2.99 Pizza: $6.99
Split cost evenly	Split cost evenly
Include tax and tip	Include tax and tip
Music Place CD: $15.00 (1/3 off) Include tax	Music Place CD: $15.00 (25% off) Include tax

*Thanks to Genni Steele, Gwen Ranzau, Nancy Hall, Nadine Cory, Michelle Skorjanec, and Brenda Sammon from White Bear Lake Public Schools, Minnesota.

The activity for Team 1 calls for fairly simple calculations using percentiles and fractions. The activity for Team 2, while similar, adds calculation of a tip (percentage), the manipulation of decimals, and the use of a percentage discount rather than fractions. More complex computations are required.

As you work on generating more complex activities, use the following questions to guide your planning.* Are students asked to:

■ identify assumptions, points of view, or problems?

■ examine and support their ideas, positions, conclusions, and perspectives?

■ formulate, hypothesize, or synthesize new ideas?

■ represent, model, or demonstrate ideas in a new way rather than simply listing, applying, or summarizing another's ideas?

■ identify implications?

■ explore "what if" scenarios or other alternative perspectives, actions, or results?

Tiered by Resources

When you choose materials at various reading levels and complexity of content, you are tiering assignments by resources. Assigning these resources to students based on their reading abilities is tiering by resources. When you steer some students to print and technology resources that feature foundational information and other students to resources that feature more sophisticated, technical, or complex information, you are tiering by resources. You are matching resources to students based on instructional need or readiness.

Sometimes you'll ask students to explore different kinds of print resources. Depending on the student, you might assign such resources as newspapers, newsletters, professional or special topic magazines, and primary sources such as diaries and journals. At other times, you might assign certain students a community mentor or expert in a particular field to use as a resource.

Students using tiered resources may be engaged in the same activity (Find at least five examples of healthy lifestyle habits), or they may be assigned activities tiered by challenge or complexity *as well as* by varied resources. For example, one flexible group may use bookmarked websites to find information about healthy lifestyles and share their ideas on a display board. Another group may use print resources such as sports or fitness magazines to analyze the presentation of healthy lifestyles and construct a display board. The whole class would then compare and contrast the ideas from both sources.

As with all differentiated activities, you need to make tiering by resources as invisible as possible. One way to do that is to form learning teams, place tiered materials in various locations in the classroom, and then simply assign teams to specific work sites. Be sure that all materials look inviting and age-appropriate. Offer all your students experiences with many kinds of resources, taking care not to lock in some students to the same sort of resource.

Remember that students differ in their basic knowledge about a topic. You may have a struggling reader who knows a lot about one of your curriculum topics because it's been an area of interest. **Build on what your students know and assign resources with their knowledge level *and* reading level in mind.** Make a point of telling students that each team is using different materials and doing particular activities so they can share what they learn with the class. This plays up collaboration and plays down distinctions among resources. (See pages 104–106 for more on making tiering invisible.)

Tiered by Outcome

Sometimes you'll want all students to use the same materials but have differentiated outcomes. That way, some students can work on more advanced applications of their learning. To tier assignments by differentiated outcomes you need a clear understanding of student readiness.

For example, after reading and discussing Martin Luther King's "I Have a Dream" speech as part of a unit on social justice, students are given the following tiered assignments:

*To read more about complexity in tier III, see Understanding by Design by Grant Wiggins and Jay McTighe, pages 100–105.

Basic task: Think about Dr. King's dream for social justice, as presented in his speech. Create a visual representation of his ideas.

Advanced task: Think about the United States today. What other dreams of social justice do you believe have surfaced in response to new issues and concerns? Create a visual representation of your ideas.

In this example, all students are building an understanding of social justice through their study of King's speech. The basic activity asks students simply to identify and illustrate King's concept of social justice. The advanced activity uses King's speech as a foundation for understanding social justice but then projects the concept onto current American society. The outcome, which involves identifying today's social justice issues, is more advanced and so is most appropriate for students with a good understanding both of King's speech and of the meaning of social justice.

Tiered by Process

At times, you'll want students to work on similar outcomes but use different processes to get there. For example, a question for a unit on consumerism might be: "How do consumers make wise buying decisions based on relevant criteria?" Here are assignments that address this question, tiered by process:

Basic task: Choose a product (for example, a DVD player) and review consumer information about it in publications such as consumer magazines. Identify relevant criteria for deciding what you should look for when purchasing this product.

Advanced task: Choose a product (for example, a DVD player) and interview at least three people who have bought it. Identify the criteria these people used in making their decision to buy.

In this example, both groups are working on the same outcome—identifying the criteria used to purchase a particular item—and both are doing research. For the basic activity, students research criteria cited in publications for consumers. For the advanced activity, students use the more advanced research process of interviewing. Students should perceive such activities as fair, since both groups are doing research. Be careful, however, that one activity doesn't demand more out-of-class time than the other. In this example, you could lessen fairness concerns by having advanced students develop their interview questions during class or find school staff or faculty to interview during school time. You might also enhance students' sense of community by having each group share results and compare the purchasing criteria people actually use to the criteria recommended in consumer publications. Students could all contribute to a class list of relevant criteria on which to base purchasing decisions.

Tiered by Product

At times, you may form groups based on learning preference, using Gardner's multiple intelligences. Assignments can then be differentiated based on product. (Keep in mind, however, that products often require more than one kind of intelligence.) For example, students might be asked to identify characteristics of effective leaders by exploring various works of historical fiction. Tiered products related to this outcome are:

Bodily/kinesthetic: Share characteristics of effective leaders through a video-recorded "Meeting of the Minds" skit, featuring characters from historical fiction that represent various leadership traits.

Visual/spatial: Share characteristics of effective leaders by constructing bulletin board displays that illustrate the leadership traits of various characters from historical fiction.

Deciding When and How to Tier an Assignment

On your curriculum maps, you considered exit points, the times when flexible groups may be necessary and helpful. The following questions can assist you in further identifying times when flexible groups and tiered assignments might be useful. Each question is followed by a recommended method for tiering.

1. Are there points when some students need more time to work on content or a skill and other students are ready for more advanced work (the exit points on your curriculum map)?

    ■ Tier by challenge

    ■ Tier by complexity

2. Is there an activity in which varied resources could be matched with student needs and readiness?

    ■ Tier by resources

3. Is there an activity in which the same materials could be used to work on both basic and more advanced outcomes?

    ■ Tier by outcome

4. Is there an activity in which students could benefit from working on the same outcome but doing different kinds of work?

    ■ Tier by process

5. Is there an activity that could result in more than one way for students to show what they've learned?

    ■ Tier by product

Guidelines for Designing Tiered Assignments

Carol Ann Tomlinson suggests that teachers picture a ladder when developing tiered assignments.[1] **You might begin your tiering process by designing a basic task for the bottom rung of the ladder and then develop activities of greater challenge or complexity.** Or you might prefer to come up with the more advanced task first, for the top of the ladder. Then you'd ask: What would be a more basic activity than this one? It doesn't matter which way you begin; what's important is that you carefully analyze each task and determine its level of difficulty.

When designing tasks that focus on different outcomes, you might think first about what you want *all* students to learn (the basic outcome related to an essential or unit question) and then think about what you expect only *some* students will learn because of its complexity, abstractness, or sophistication (the advanced outcome related to the essential or unit question). When designing activities tiered by process or product, you simply need to be aware of the different ways students prefer to learn and demonstrate their learning (learning styles, Gardner's multiple intelligences). **To ease your workload, you might develop tiered assignments in collaboration with another teacher,** as described in Chapter 5 (pages 95–96).

You can also begin tiering by reviewing what might already be provided in your teacher's edition of a textbook. Look at a given unit's assignments and exercises. What is their level of challenge or complexity? What's already there might give you a start on a tiered assignment. Design a more advanced activity if the one given is basic; if the one given is advanced, design a more basic activity. As you review your teacher's edition, use these questions to mine ideas for tiered assignments:

1. Are there two activities or two versions of one activity that could be combined to create a tiered assignment at basic and more advanced levels? (For example, some math texts provide two ways to play a game, one easy and one more difficult.)

2. Is there an activity at a basic level? Or is there an activity at an advanced level? Use what's there and provide the level that's missing.

---

[1] *The Differentiated Classroom* by Carol Ann Tomlinson (Alexandria, VA: Association for Supervision and Curriculum Development, 1999).

3. Have you used an assignment with students that proved too difficult for some students? That's your advanced tier.

4. Have you used an assignment with students that proved too easy for some students? That's your basic tier.

How to Organize Groups and Give Directions

How do you set up teams and give directions to the various groups doing tiered activities? At the beginning of class or group time, you might simply list teams and their members on the board or a flip chart.

You can also use a pocket chart. Write the name of each student on the front of an index card. Sort the cards in alphabetical order and number them consecutively on the back. As you form learning teams, place the name cards of each team's members under the learning team card (for example, Team 1) in the pocket chart. When the activity is completed, put the cards in numerical order (which is also alphabetical order). Now you can quickly deal out new teams for another tiered activity without digging through the pile hunting for names.

At times, you may wish to set up tiered assignments at workstations, using tables or desks pushed together. Equip each workstation with all necessary materials. Direct students to the appropriate group and then provide them with workcards that explain the assignment, procedures, and assessment criteria.

Workcards

A handy way to provide directions for each tiered assignment is to create workcards using index cards or half- or full-sized sheets of paper. Number, letter, label, or color-code the cards to indicate the team or group they're written for (for example, the red team gets a red card). Distribute the cards to students directly or place them at each group's workstation. If you'll be using the cards repeatedly, laminate them or slide them into clear, plastic sheet protectors. Here are some examples of tiered assignments presented on workcards.

FIGURE 13

Workcards (Solar System)
Grade 3

Workcard

Green Team

Carefully review your books and bookmarked websites. Each group member should select a different planet to study. Do the following activities:

On your own:

1. List the planets in order from the sun. Write one new fact you learned about each planet.

2. On construction paper, sketch the planets in order of size, from largest to smallest.

3. Complete a chart listing how the planet you chose is like and not like Earth.

With your work team:

Plan and present a skit about why each of you would like to visit and explore the planet you chose.

Workcard

Purple Team

Carefully review your science magazines and bookmarked websites. Each group member should select a different planet to study. Do the following activities:

On your own:

1. Write three facts about the planet you chose that weren't included in our classroom study.

2. Write two questions about the planet you chose that science hasn't answered yet. (What is still a mystery about the planet?)

With a partner from your work team:

Decide whether your planet or your partner's planet would be best for the United States to explore and possibly settle. Prepare a class presentation about your decision and the reasons for your choice. Create a visual aid to use in your presentation.

F I G U R E   1 4

Workcards (Cultural/Ethnic Studies)
Middle School or High School

Workcard

Blue Team

We have examined both voluntary and involuntary immigration to America. Check the immigrant group below that you will research for your project*:

❑ Africans (voluntary immigrants)
The African nation I will study:_____

❑ Africans (involuntary immigrants)
The African nation I will study:_____

❑ Europeans
The European country I will study:_____

❑ Hispanics/Chicanos/Latinos
The Hispanic/Chicano/Latino
country that I will study:_____

❑ Asians
The Asian country I will study:_____

❑ Arabs
The Arabic country I will study: _____

Using available media center resources, including CD-ROMs and the Internet, do the following:

1. Identify the reasons for your group's immigration to the United States.

2. Create a time line of key events in the history of this group's life in America.

3. Create a Hall of Fame of notable Americans from this group and their contributions to American life.

Use a trifold display board for your information. Develop a creative class presentation to share the results of your team's research.

Workcard

Red Team

We have examined both voluntary and involuntary immigration to America. Check the immigrant group below that you will research for your project:

❑ Africans (voluntary immigrants)
The African nation I will study:_____

❑ Africans (involuntary immigrants)
The African nation I will study:_____

❑ Europeans
The European country I will study:_____

❑ Hispanics/Chicanos/Latinos
The Hispanic/Chicano/Latino
country that I will study:_____

❑ Asians
The Asian country I will study:_____

❑ Arabs
The Arabic country I will study: _____

Using available media center resources, including CD-ROMs and the Internet, do the following:

1. Identify the discriminatory factors faced by this group, as well as actions the group took to challenge discrimination.

2. Describe the group's general degree of assimilation into mainstream American culture (include language, evidence of communities, and sense of cultural/ethnic identity). What factors may have assisted or hindered their assimilation?

3. Identify the group's current economic status in America and determine factors that may have contributed to this status.

Develop a class presentation of the results of your research, in the style of a news magazine, that includes role-played interviews.

*There are both national and regional preferences about the naming of cultural and ethnic groups. If you choose to use this example activity, please adjust the language as needed. For more information about cultural/ethnic studies, see *Teaching Strategies for Ethnic Studies* by James A. Banks (Boston: Allyn & Bacon, 2008).

Warm-Ups and Cool-Downs

To provide some time to work with each flexible group, you may wish to use warm-ups and cool-downs. Warm-ups and cool-downs are short, routine activities that demand little or no direction from you. You may wish to start a class period with warm-ups to get flexible groups underway and then use cool-downs as activities your students turn to when they finish assignments early.

Using warm-ups at the beginning of a class period gives you time to provide more instruction or introduce directions to one group and then move on to the second group. Start by forming your groups, then direct one group to the warm-ups while you provide additional instruction or directions for the tiered activity to the second group. Then "flip" the groups. While you give directions to the first group, the second group gets underway with its tiered assignment. The second group goes to the warm-up at the end of the class period when its tiered assignment is complete.

Here are some examples of common warm-ups and cool-downs:

■ Journaling

■ Free reading

■ Skill applications or challenges

■ Sketchbooks

■ Notetaking on text chapters or articles

■ Content webs

■ Logic problems or puzzlers

■ Word-of-the-day

■ Creative thinking activities

■ Daily oral language

It's important that students not view warm-ups or cool-downs as busywork or time fillers. These activities might consist of work that you've routinely assigned and are now using either before and after students work in groups.

In the next chapter, you will be introduced to project menus (pages 111–113) and challenge centers (pages 113–115). These differentiated activities can also be used as warm-ups or cool-downs to assure that students are always involved in relevant, worthwhile learning.

Making Tiering Invisible

The more variety you use with instructional grouping, the more students accept such work teams as the norm in your classroom. With a variety of grouping and instructional strategies, tiered assignments and flexible instructional groups seem less noticeable and less novel for kids. A supportive classroom environment is also critical to your success in differentiating instruction. Review the characteristics of such an environment in Chapter 1, page 13.

From time to time, it's important to use cooperative learning groups, student-selected groups, and groups based on learning preferences and special interests. Students with varying abilities need opportunities to work together. Keep in mind that the membership of flexible groups is fluid. Even your advanced learners sometimes will need more time on some skills or content. Few students are equally talented in all subject areas. Similarly, students who are most frequently assigned reteaching activities may do well with advanced assignments in their areas of special interest or experience. When you make it a point to get to know your students' strengths, preferences, and interests, you can more successfully differentiate their instruction.

Make sure you introduce all tiered activities in an equally enthusiastic manner and alternate which activity is introduced first. Also, take some time to think of neutral ways to name learning teams. Try numbering them (Team 1), using color codes (Yellow Team), or even calling teams by one member's name (Damon's Team). Vary the teams' task assignments so that Team 1, for example, doesn't always get the advanced activity.

Here are criteria and examples for making tiered assignments less visible to students. Use them to see if your assignments will measure up to your students' scrutiny. Tiered assignments should be:

Different work, not simply more or less work. The following "advanced task" isn't really more advanced. It's just more work and will be perceived as such by students:

> **Basic task:** Read two American short stories set in the 20th century and compare and contrast them on a chart.

> **Advanced task:** Read three American short stories set in the 20th century and compare and contrast them on a chart.

Here's how this assignment could be differentiated:

> **Basic task:** Read two American short stories set in the 20th century and compare and contrast them on a chart.

> **Advanced task:** Read two American short stories set in the 20th century and determine how each story might be told if it were set during this millennium. What would be the same? What would be different? Why? Share your ideas on a chart.

Equally active. Students will be justifiably unhappy if one activity involves active learning, such as a role play or debate, and the other activity is a paper-and-pencil task. **Plan activities that, while different, allow the same level of activity.** Of course, if you're grouping by product or learning preference, one group may indeed be best-suited and happiest making a chart and the other delighted with performing a skit.

Equally interesting and engaging. Think about your assignments from the students' perspective. If one calls for drill and practice and the other calls for a creative group activity (such as a simulation), which would you choose? **You need to make activities equally desirable so students won't feel they're being treated unfairly.** Interesting and engaging activities offer another benefit: they are much more likely to motivate students.

Fair in terms of work expectations. The following two assignments are not well designed:

> **Basic task:** Use your text and class notes to create a visual way to illustrate key facts about cells. Include our vocabulary words and the topics and issues we studied related to cell biology.

> **Advanced task:** Research a current topic or issue related to cell biology that we did not discuss in class. Create a visual way to inform us about the topic.

Students assigned the advanced task would immediately question why they're expected to do research while other students are simply collecting information from the text and their notes. Although the tasks may respond to differences in content knowledge—the students assigned the basic task are being rerouted through foundational content while the advanced students are being introduced to new content—the assignments *feel* unfair.

Think about the work time needed to complete each of your tiered assignments. Are the time commitments comparable? Tasks can be different, based on instructional need, yet comparable in the time and effort needed to complete them successfully. For example:

> **Basic task:** Using your text and class notes, create either a visual or a musical way (a poster or a rap) to illustrate important vocabulary words related to cells.

> **Advanced task:** Using your text and class notes, invent a way to help others remember the work of the cell. Include important aspects of its purpose and functions related to the human body. Come up with a rap, poster, riddle, or rock song to tell your cell's story.

Require the use of key concepts, skills, or ideas. When you ask students to carry out tiered assignments, you should, at a minimum, be asking them to use what they know or are learning. Such assignments constitute the wisest use of students' class time. Higher-level tasks (at Bloom's apply, analyze, evaluate, or create levels), by their very nature, tend to be more engaging for students than tasks at the knowledge and comprehension levels.

If you think about these criteria while planning tiered assignments for flexible instructional groups, you'll be much more likely to design fair, equitable activities. The next chapter describes ways to allow student choice with tiered activities.

CHAPTER 7

What Do Students Need?
Choices

Grouping students and prescribing tiered assignments based on students' learning needs is the essence of differentiated instruction. However, most teachers agree that there is value in offering students choices about what and how they'll learn. **Offering choices is an important way to motivate students and get them interested in a project.** Even with the tiered activities you prescribe for particular groups, you can often allow students some degree of choice. For example, you might assign a basic task but offer group members a choice of process (such as reading or interviewing) and/or product (such as a booklet, a skit, or an illustration).

This chapter presents four strategies for providing student choice within tiered assignments: pathways plans, project menus, challenge centers, and spin-offs. See which options answer your specific curricular or classroom needs. As explained in the introduction, a goal of this book is to present lots of ways you can "go at" differentiation. You deserve choices as much as your students do. Use what appeals to you and seems best for helping your students learn.

Pathways Plans

Pathways plans provide a format for keeping track of students' skill development and presenting a choice of tiered, alternative activities to students who demonstrate proficiency in a particular skill. Pathways help you manage assignments when you're using a procedure called instructional looping.

Instructional Looping

Differentiating according to skill proficiency is called *looping.* Students "loop" in and out of skill instruction according to their learning needs. Looping is another way to approach flexible grouping on a day-to-day basis, allowing you to provide direct skill instruction to those who need

it and alternative activities for students who have particular skills well in hand. Here's how it works.

Students work with you as you provide instruction on skills they need. Those who master the skills quickly, or those who have demonstrated proficiency on a preassessment, loop out of instruction to work on tiered assignments they choose from pathways plans. **Looping is an effective strategy to use at exit points in your curriculum, when student readiness varies significantly.** Looping and pathways plans are particularly useful at the beginning of a school year when some of our instructional time may be devoted to review and practice of last year's skills. At the beginning of a unit, it's helpful to plan alternative activities for students who will loop out of skills instruction. Then you won't have to ask yourself each day: What am I going to do with kids who don't need this skill instruction?

The First Step: Preassessment

As discussed in Chapter 2, finding out about your students includes discovering what they know by means of preassessments. You can offer preassessments at the beginning of the year or on a unit-by-unit or skill-by-skill basis.

Marissa Sanchez, an experienced fifth-grade teacher, is getting ready to begin her first math unit of the school year. She's pretty sure that some of her students are already proficient in one or more of this unit's skills. She also knows that, as the unit goes on, some students will need more instruction, time, and practice than others.

Marissa reviews the math skills competency checklists (provided by the fourth-grade teachers) looking for skills that students have already been taught and that are required in her first unit. For students new to the school, she pulls sample problems from the end-of-the-unit review exercises (provided in her teacher's guide) and uses them as a skills preassessment.

Preassessment can take many forms. It can be a pencil-and-paper pretest or information from skills checklists, portfolios, or daily assignments. If you use pretests, offer them to all students, telling them which skills you'll be testing and when the preassessment will be given. It may surprise you how many students tote textbooks home to prepare for preassessments! Many students welcome the opportunity to "test out" and earn the right to choose alternative pathways projects.

Decide what standard you will consider mastery or proficiency; many teachers use 85 percent to 90 percent as the standard. Here's an example of a simple math preassessment developed from an end-of-unit activity in a textbook:

Identifying Factors and Prime and Composite Numbers

10 points (Mastery level = 8 out of 10)

For each number, list all the factors. Then indicate whether the number is a prime or composite number.

Number	Factors	Prime or Composite?
3		
8		
15		
23		
28		

Creating Pathways Plans

As you can see in the following samples (pages 109–110), pathways are individual planners on which you or your students check off or cross out the skills they've mastered and choose from a list of alternative activities. To create pathways, list your unit's skills (from your curriculum map) on the left side of a sheet of paper. On the right side, list alternative activities that students can choose from when they loop out of skills instruction. Be sure to include some short-term projects for students who loop out of instruction for only one or two class sessions.

Marissa knows she needs to plan activities for students who have looped out of instruction on a particular math skill. Using her experience in designing tiered assignments, the challenge activities provided in her teacher's edition, and enrichment materials provided by her school, she plans "instead of" activities for these students.

In developing pathways, be sure to tier the activities according to challenge level or by complexity (see Chapter 6, pages 97–99). If you're using a textbook series, you might start by examining activities designated as "challenge," "enrichment," or "for advanced learners." Decide for yourself whether these are truly challenging or just more of the same. Some activities labeled "advanced" are actually low level. Look through enrichment materials you may have used before and consider websites or software that might be used to extend or enrich the curriculum. Take care not to stray from your essential and unit questions. Ask yourself: How can students go more deeply into this topic?

Figures 15 and 16, page 109, are two examples of pathways, one for seventh-grade language arts and one for fifth-grade math. The language arts example shows projects related not to the unit (grammar and sentence structure) but to the curricular area (language arts). Since students didn't need to spend more time on grammar activities, projects were designed using books students were reading during sustained silent reading time in the classroom. The math example shows alternative activities that are directly related to the unit: number theory. Note that the "design your own project" option (as shown on both examples) is a useful final project choice.

FIGURE 15

Language Arts Pathways: Grammar and Sentence Structure Grade 7

Skills

Identification of:

- [ ] Nouns
- [ ] Adverbs
- [ ] Pronouns
- [ ] Prepositional phrases
- [ ] Verbs
- [ ] Adjectives
- [ ] Conjunctions
- [ ] Subject/predicate

Sentence types:

- [ ] Compound sentences
- [ ] Fragments/run-ons

Word choice:

- [ ] Subject/verb agreement
- [ ] Verb tense

Select from these book projects:

1. Choose and analyze a scene from your book. If you were a film director, how would you present the action? Create specific, detailed plans on a storyboard and in a written summary.

2. Pretend you've been asked to write a letter of recommendation for one of the book's characters who wants a job. Include a description of the character's personal traits, strengths, and limitations.

3. Compose a conversation between yourself and a character in the book. What would you ask this person or discuss? What would you want to know? What would you want to say? Write out both your dialogue and the character's dialogue, or write a script for the conversation and audio record it with a partner.

4. Determine a new solution for a problem presented in the book. Identify possible consequences of this change for characters and for subsequent action in the story. Create a flowchart of the implications.

5. Provide a new solution for a problem faced by a character. Present your solution as a response in an advice column.

6. Write a review of the book as a columnist for a newspaper's arts section. Discuss plot, theme, and character development. Present your opinions about the book, with supporting evidence. Critique the author's ability to tell a story.

7. Create a scrapbook or collection of illustrations of significant events from the book. Include notes or comments as if written by one of the characters.

8. If this book were being made into a film, what would you choose as the theme song? Record the song and explain on the recording why it's a good musical statement of the book and movie's theme.

9. Design your own book project. See me before you start.

FIGURE 16

Math Pathways: Number Theory Grade 5

Skills

- [ ] Squaring numbers
- [ ] Identifying factors
- [ ] Identifying multiples
- [ ] Identifying prime and composite numbers
- [ ] Identifying even and odd numbers
- [ ] Identifying divisibility
- [ ] Constructing rectangular arrays

Select from these activities:

1. Create a mind map that will help someone remember number theory.

2. Develop a die or spinner game using prime/composite or even/odd numbers.

3. Design a string of math operations whose answer is 128. Use a combination of any of the following: squaring numbers, identifying multiples, and identifying factors.

4. Create a "Guess My Number" booklet, using any of the following as clues: squaring, factoring, multiples, prime/composite, even/odd, and divisibility.

5. Create a math rap or rhyme that will help someone remember a concept from number theory (for example, how to square numbers).

6. Design your own project using number theory. See me before you start.

For purposes of space, you may need to write an abbreviated activity description on the pathways sheet and then give students a workcard (see Chapter 6, pages 102–103) with more detailed directions or procedures. It's also helpful to include a checklist of criteria for them to evaluate their work. The following figure shows a workcard for the third project on the language arts pathways sheet: "Compose a conversation between yourself and a character in the book."

F I G U R E   1 7

Workcard (Project 3)

Workcard

Compose a conversation between yourself and a character in the book. What would you ask this character or discuss with him or her? What would you want to know? What would you want to say? Write out both your dialogue and the character's dialogue, or write a script for the conversation and audio record it with a partner.

1. Choose a character from the book to have a conversation with.

2. Imagine what you would ask the character or talk about:

   ■ Would you talk about something in the plot of the book?

   ■ Would you want to know more about the character's likes, dislikes, and experiences?

   ■ Is there something that puzzles you about this character or others in the book that you would like to ask about?

   ■ Is there something unresolved or undecided in the book that you would like to know more about?

   ■ Do you want to know the character's perspective or opinion about something that happened in the story?

   ■ What else would you like to discuss with the character?

3. Choose *one* of the following:

   a. Write the conversation, including both your dialogue and the character's dialogue.

   b. Write a script of the conversation and audio record it with a partner.

Evaluation checklist for the conversation or script

❑ Includes topics based on the plot and action of the book.

❑ Provides enough detail so that the responses of the character can be clearly understood.

❑ Conveys the character's probable responses, based on the story.

❑ Uses appropriate grammar, punctuation, and capitalization.

❑ Uses correct spelling.

❑ Shows correct word choice and verb tense.

Quality criteria for audio recording

❑ Is clear and loud enough to be understood.

Management Procedures for Pathways Plans

Distribute pathways plans to all students or only to those who loop out of at least one skill. Here are nine steps for managing pathways plans:

1. You may have students check off or cross out the skills they master on their pathways plan. For example, students who got 8, 9, or 10 correct on the pretest for prime and composite numbers (page 108) would cross out "identifying prime and composite numbers" from the list on the math pathways example (page 109). Or you may simply decide to refer to your gradebook or records and list the students who are to loop out for that session at the beginning of the class period.

2. Students move to the appropriate activity for the class period. Those who have not pretested out of a particular skill stay with you for direct instruction, reteaching, or further practice. Students who have demonstrated mastery of the skill select an activity from the pathways plan.

3. All students are responsible for their daily work. Those with you are responsible for whatever activity or assignment you give them related to the skill being taught. Those doing pathways projects are responsible for completing that activity in lieu of the skill work.

4. Students who are looping out of skill instruction for more than one class session should be encouraged to choose from more complex projects that require more than one class session to complete.

5. Ask students who have looped out to rejoin the group you're instructing when you've moved beyond simple drill and practice of the skill or when you're moving into presentation of new content or skills.

6. Have materials needed for pathways projects available at a workstation—for example, a countertop, table, or cluster of desks. (For more ideas on how to manage differentiated tasks and their materials, see Chapter 9.)

7. You may find it convenient to give students a file folder or hanging file in which to keep their pathways plans and all work in progress.

8. As work is completed, students turn it in for grading. Grades on pathways projects replace grades on skill work done by the other students. You'll need to negotiate with some students the number and extent of pathways projects required. Those students looping out of instruction for several days during a unit would have different requirements than those looping out only once or twice. Naturally, "done-in-a-day" assignments are weighted less heavily than more comprehensive activities that require multiple class sessions. For example, students who looped out of four skills lessons during a unit would be expected to do more than one activity from the pathways plan.

9. Since it's likely that some students won't qualify to loop out of any skills sessions, consider giving all students an opportunity to choose a pathways project during one class period.

Project Menus

A project menu is a numbered list of tiered assignments that can be used for a variety of purposes in a differentiated classroom. When you present tiered assignments to students on a project menu, you allow them to choose what they'd like to work on. You develop the tiered assignments based on challenge. Some activities are more basic, calling on the recall, understand, and apply levels of Bloom's taxonomy. Others are more advanced, focusing on the analyze, evaluate, or create levels. You design menu activities so that students can present their learning in a variety of ways.

Project menus can be used in several ways:

- as a choice of required projects related to a curricular unit.

- as warm-up activities for flexible instructional groups. (See Warm-Ups and Cool-Downs in Chapter 6, page 104.)

- as cool-down activities that students can work on when they finish assignments before the class period ends.

- as an alternative to pathways plans for students who have looped out of skills instruction.

- as a list of activities that all students choose from at particular times during your unit ("Menu Days").

If you decide to offer project menu activities only to those students who complete their work early, plan some brief activities and others that may take more time. Also, think about how you can fairly recognize students who do projects from the menus without penalizing other students who need all their class time for assigned work. What might encourage students to complete project menu activities, yet not discourage other students who can't spare the class time to do them?

Developing Project Menus

As you design menu activities, be sure to refer to your essential and unit questions. You may find it helpful to construct your project menu on a blank matrix plan (pages 86–87), which supplies verbs for each level of Bloom's taxonomy, or on an integration matrix (pages 88–89), which supplies verbs for Bloom's levels as well as suggested Gardner-based products. The following sample matrix plan shows project menu activities for a unit on folktales and fairy tales. As you can see, menus should include at least one activity at each of Bloom's levels, but have a greater number of activities at the apply level and higher so that students will have sufficient challenge.

F I G U R E   1 8

Matrix Plan Used to Design a Project Menu

Unit/Theme: Folktales and fairy tales

Unit Questions:

What are the characteristics of folktales and fairy tales?
What are repeating patterns or themes used in folktales and fairy tales?
How is factual information represented in this genre?
How are lessons taught or morals presented in folktales and fairy tales?
What are some cross-cultural stories or themes found in folktales and fairy tales?

Bloom's Taxonomy

Recall	Understand	Apply	Analyze	Evaluate	Create
tell, list, define, label, recite, memorize, repeat, find, name, record, fill in, recall, relate	*locate, explain, summarize, identify, describe, report, discuss, review, paraphrase, restate, retell, show, outline, rewrite*	*demonstrate, construct, record, use, diagram, revise, reformat, illustrate, interpret, dramatize, practice, organize, translate, manipulate, convert, adapt, research, calculate, operate, model, order, display, implement, sequence, integrate, incorporate*	*compare, contrast, classify, critique, solve, deduce, examine, differentiate, appraise, distinguish, experiment, question, investigate, categorize, infer*	*judge, predict, verify, assess, justify, rate, prioritize, determine, decide, value, forecast, estimate*	*compose, hypothesize, design, formulate, create, invent, develop, refine, produce, transform*
Read about wolves in reference books or on our bookmarked websites. Review the fairy tales we've read that have wolves as characters. Make a chart listing facts and fiction (true/false information) about wolves, or create a collection of items or artifacts to represent your ideas about wolves, whether fact or fiction.	Make a list of the heroes and villains in the fairy tales we've read in class and those you've read on your own. Explain why you consider each a hero or a villain by creating picture book illustrations or a rap or jingle.	Retell a folktale or fairy tale of your choice on an illustrated timeline. Include a minimum of four events. Write a journal entry about a day in the life of a folktale or fairy tale character. Include details from the story.	Pretend that a villain in a folktale or fairy tale is going on trial. Decide if you will defend or prosecute this villain. Write testimony that could be used in a trial to prove the villain's guilt or innocence. Include information about what caused the villain to go bad and what led to his or her actions in the story. Record or act out your testimony. Compare and contrast two versions of a fairy tale, one from Grimm's Fairy Tales and one from another culture. Chart how the versions are alike and different.	If you could have a magic power like the characters in fairy tales, what power would you choose and how would you use it? Show yourself and your new power by making a poster, telling a story, writing a song or rap, or doing a skit.	Retell a folktale or fairy tale from the villain's perspective. Share your story by creating a comic strip.

FIGURE 19

Project Menu: Sample

Topic: Folktales and fairy tales

1. Read about wolves in reference books or on our bookmarked websites. Review the fairy tales we've read that have wolves as characters. Make a chart that lists facts and fiction (true/false information) about wolves, or create a collection of items or artifacts to represent your ideas about wolves, whether fact or fiction.

2. If you could have a magic power like the characters in fairy tales, what power would you choose and how would you use it? Show yourself and your new power by making a poster, telling a story, writing a song or rap, or doing a skit.

3. Make a list of the heroes and villains in the fairy tales we've read in class and those you've read on your own. Explain why you consider each a hero or a villain by creating picture book illustrations or a rap or jingle.

4. Pretend that a villain in a folktale or fairy tale is going on trial. Decide whether you will defend or prosecute this villain. Write testimony that could be used in a trial to prove the villain's guilt or innocence. Include information about what caused the villain to go bad and what led to his or her actions in the story. Record or act out your testimony.

5. Retell a folktale or fairy tale of your choice on an illustrated timeline. Include at least four events.

6. Retell a folktale or fairy tale from the villain's perspective. Share your story by creating a comic strip.

7. Write a journal entry about a day in the life of a folktale or fairy tale character. Include details from the story.

8. Compare and contrast two versions of a fairy tale, one from *Grimm's Fairy Tales* and one from another culture. Chart how the versions are alike and different.

Guidelines for Project Menus

When creating your project menu, consider coding the projects you've designed so you can more easily guide students toward particular projects. For example, you can list more challenging activities (analyze, evaluate, create) on even numbers and more basic activities (recall, understand, apply) on the odd numbers. It's probably best not to tell students how you've coded the activities. You want to encourage the struggling student who is excited about an even-numbered project to do that project. You don't want to discourage kids from their selections based on how you've categorized activities, and you don't want students teased because they choose from the more challenging, even-numbered projects. If you adhere to the guidelines for making tiered assignments invisible (see Chapter 6, pages 104–106), you'll find your students more open to possibilities.

Don't hesitate to be prescriptive with students who need more direction. Intervene when you want to ensure that a particular student chooses an appropriately differentiated task. Recommend modifications or adaptations that make activities more suitable to the abilities, talents, and learning needs of a particular student. For example, if you have students who tend to choose less challenging assignments although they're capable of doing more, you may wish to encourage them (privately) to choose from even-numbered activities. You're still offering choices, but you're steering them toward activities best suited to their needs. You might simply decide to require that students check with you after they've made their project choices.

As with pathways plans, it's helpful to use workcards to provide more specific directions for particular projects. Include checklists with quality criteria so that students clearly understand your expectations and can maintain high standards.

Challenge Centers

Another way you can provide students with a choice of tiered assignments and encourage them to work independently is by creating challenge centers. **Challenge centers provide a differentiated twist on a frequently used management strategy: learning centers or stations.** They can be used with any subject area, and by students at any grade level, to extend and enrich a curricular unit. As you can see in Figure 20 on page 115 (activities for an elementary-level unit on insects), challenge center projects stress new concepts, new content, or the application of skills.

You can also design challenge centers to focus on multiple intelligences. A logical/mathematical center, for example, would include projects involving charts, graphs, or puzzles related to your unit of study. Activities at a verbal/linguistic center would encourage storytelling, writing, or research. A visual/spatial center would provide materials and ideas for political cartoons, posters, models, or storyboards. A bodily/kinesthetic center might be an inventor's lab. Again, students are given an opportunity to choose the activity they wish to pursue.

Use challenge centers:

- as a regular part of your unit, giving all students Challenge Center Days to select from these curriculum-enrichment activities.

- as another way to present alternative activities for instructional looping.

- for warm-ups, giving you time to get a flexible group underway.

- for cool-downs, to engage students in worthwhile activities when they complete their assigned work early.

Guidelines for Challenge Centers

Keep in mind that one of the purposes of challenge centers is to encourage students to work independently. Consider the following guidelines:

1. As with all differentiated assignments, develop activities that relate to your essential and unit questions. Focus on significant learning outcomes.

2. Since challenge centers are for all students, design activities with the level of challenge or complexity in mind. Will this be a foundational or an advanced activity? Will this activity reinforce content or introduce new material?

3. Use a variety of materials and activities that respond to a wide range of reading levels, learning preferences, levels of challenge and complexity, and student interests.

4. Decide which activities will be done individually and which may be done with a partner or small group.

5. Include short-term (done-in-a-day) activities as well as multiple-session projects.

6. Provide step-by-step procedures on workcards. Think about what steps students will need to follow to successfully complete the activity independently.

7. Design evaluation checklists for projects. What will characterize high-quality work? *Before* the project is turned in to you, ask students to do a self-evaluation and have a classmate do a peer evaluation using the checklist.

8. Provide needed materials and/or resources.

9. To help students be accountable for their time, have them use a worklog to record the work they accomplish each day in challenge centers. (Photocopy the sample form on page 118.) Staple the worklog into a folder or hanging file. A quick look will enable you to easily monitor their progress.

10. Provide examples, samples, or models as necessary to explain assignments.

11. Organize workcards, evaluation checklists, and materials so that students can work independently.

Materials and resources for centers need to be organized and readily available for student use. A section on your countertop, a tabletop, an extra student desk or two, or materials in bins will work. Some teachers set up challenge centers using the plastic shoe or sweater boxes available in closet supply departments. A workcard, an evaluation checklist, and all materials are packed in the box, along with a check-in list. The check-in list reminds students of what needs to be repacked in the box so that it is ready for the next user. You may wish to laminate the workcard and tape it inside the lid. You can also use index cards for workcards, quality criteria, and check-in lists, putting a metal ring or brass fastener through the cards to keep them together in the box. This works especially well if you're short on space, since students can take the box to their own desk or table. Label your boxes by activity and stack them on shelves or countertop.

Start small. Develop just a couple of challenge centers. Develop more centers for subsequent units as you learn what does and doesn't work with your particular students. Keep your curriculum goals in mind, as well as topics your students may be interested in. You don't need challenge centers for every unit or topic, just those that seem appropriate for relevant extension or enrichment. And don't hesitate to use ready-to-go activities from websites, computer software, curriculum guides, or materials guides.

FIGURE 20

Suggested Activities for a Challenge Center on Insects

1. Read *Two Bad Ants* by Carl Van Allsburg (Houghton Mifflin, 1988). Write a story or create a comic strip describing the obstacles and adventures of two ants, like the ones in Van Allsburg's story, who are living in your school or home.

2. Create "baseball cards" for an insect of your choice. Give your insect a nickname to identify a specific characteristic (for example, "Hairy" or "Skitter"). Include "stats" on your insect for the back of the card, including its size and other physical features.

3. Create a contribution to a museum featuring newly discovered insects.

■ Construct a model or sketch of your new insect.

■ Create a field guide entry for your new insect that includes:

common name

scientific name

physical features

life span

eating habits

characteristics that make it an insect

4. Construct a Venn diagram comparing and contrasting

■ bees and wasps

■ butterflies and moths

■ spiders and centipedes

5. Review the books and bookmarked websites at the center and add to our class chart by categorizing insects as helpful, harmful, or pesky.

6. Determine what insect characteristic you might like to have and why. Create an invention that will enable people to have that characteristic. Draw an ad or make a model of your invention. Be sure to name your invention and describe how to use it.

7. Identify the insect that you believe is most valuable to humans. Create a rap, invent new lyrics for a song, or devise a campaign poster to persuade us about your choice.

Spin-Offs

Spin-offs are projects based on student interests. They may be done independently, with partners, or in small groups. You can structure them in various ways, but each allows some degree of student choice. For each kind of spin-off, you provide the general topic, which will usually be related to a specific unit or part of your curriculum. From there, you may provide as much or as little direction about content, process, and product as you wish. (A reproducible spin-off form is provided on page 119.) Here are three different ways of structuring spin-off activities.

Teacher-Directed Spin-Off

For teacher-directed spin-offs, you require that certain content or key ideas be included. The example, Figure 21, page 116, shows an art history project in which the teacher asks students to chose a particular art style and artist as their topic. The teacher has listed four requirements for content and has provided examples of products for students to pick from. If you include product examples, be sure to vary them based on learning preference or modality. Review Projects, Presentations, Performances in Chapter 2 (pages 34–38) for various products related to Gardner's multiple intelligences.

FIGURE 21

Sample: Teacher-Directed Spin-Off

General topic: Art History

What is your specific topic?

■ Choose a style of art and an artist associated with this style.

What content or key ideas will you include?

■ Years when this style of art was being produced
■ Key elements of the style
■ Biography of the artist you've chosen
■ The artist's most significant works

How will you share your work?

Project ideas:
■ Essay or research paper
■ Illustrated time line
■ Audiovisual presentation
■ Poster
■ Magazine article
■ Critique
■ Scrapbook
■ Original song or rap
■ Storytelling
■ Diagram or chart
■ Storyboard
■ Skit
■ Journal or diary of the artist
■ Scripted, audio-recorded interview
■ Collection of sketches
■ PowerPoint presentation
■ Other (please see me)

Spin-Offs with Required Product

In a spin-off with a required product, students choose their specific topic and the content or key ideas they'll include, while you assign the product that students will produce. Use this format

when you want all students to do a particular kind of project or when a project is required by your curriculum or performance assessments. The example in Figure 22 shows a science fair project to be presented on a display board. The teacher has included an evaluation checklist for students.

FIGURE 22

Sample: Spin-Off with Required Product

General topic: Science Fair exhibit

What is your specific topic? _____

What content or key ideas will you include?
_____
_____
_____

Required product: display board

Evaluation checklist

❑ Presents accurate information about your topic.
❑ Presents information clearly so the reader can learn about your topic.
❑ Includes graphics such as illustrations, charts, or graphs.
❑ Lists a minimum of three references.
❑ Reflects careful planning and layout; presents a polished appearance.

Student-Directed Spin-Offs

When students choose their own specific topic, content, and product, spin-offs become open-ended and more clearly put students in charge. The general topic you supply may reflect a theme of your curriculum, such as "exploration of the New World," or simply a subject area (such as social studies). As with teacher-directed spin-offs, you might supply a list of project ideas that includes a good variety of Gardner-based products. You can create the evaluation checklist, or work with students to create one specially tailored to their activities.

Student-directed spin-offs are the most flexible formats for these projects. They allow students to differentiate their own instruction by making independent decisions about what they'll work on and how they'll share their work. Although appropriate for all learners, this kind of spin-off may particularly appeal to your more independent, creative students and to gifted and talented learners.

Guidelines for Spin-Offs

Spin-offs provide an opportunity for you to differentiate instruction by allowing students to make some decisions about what and how they will learn. The purpose of these projects is to extend and enrich curriculum, for all students, in response to their interests. For that reason, it is best to allow class time for spin-offs, rather than assigning them as homework or adding them to your regular course requirements for advanced students. Instead, use them as part of a unit or as a culminating activity, setting aside particular days for students to work on them. If you use spin-offs as a strategy to differentiate instruction for gifted and talented students, use them instead of, rather than in addition to, other course requirements. (For more on "instead of" projects for gifted and talented learners, see pages 141–145 in Chapter 10.)

It would not be unusual to find that many students select too broad a topic for study. To help them narrow down their project, ask them to do some "reading around the topic." (See page 120 for a useful form.) Notice that students are asked to keep track of the resources they consult. Then, as they narrow their topic, they can return to specific resources.

Once students have decided on a topic, it's helpful to provide a format for them to record the resources they actually use. See Resources Log, page 121, for a handout you can supply.

Depending on the kind of spin-off you assign, students need to make several decisions. They must decide on their specific topic and how they will research key concepts and ideas. They must decide how and where they will gather information. For some spin-offs, they must decide how they will show what they've learned. It's helpful to give students a planning form so they can keep track of their work. Distribute the Project Planner and Checklist on page 122. Establish due dates for each step of the project.

To help with your own record keeping and to encourage students to be accountable for their work, staple a copy of the Worklog form (see page 118) to the front of a file folder that holds each student's spin-off work in progress. Give students the responsibility to complete this log after each class work session. That way you can quickly and easily review students' daily work. Remember to build in some time at the end of a class period for students to fill out their worklogs.

You'll also need to develop evaluation checklists that reflect your specific criteria for spin-off projects. Ask students to attach this sheet to their spin-off form and to use the criteria to guide their work. Checklists can also be used by students for self-evaluation after a project is done. You might suggest that students conduct peer reviews using the evaluation checklist so that projects can be revised or modified before they're turned in to you.

At the end of spin-off projects, you may also wish to have students complete a self-reflection activity that asks them to consider what they learned. See Self-Reflection on page 123 for an example you could distribute. This form, as well as others in this chapter, can also be used with other kinds of projects or activities.

Worklog

Name: _____

Today: Note specific information about today's accomplishments: page numbers read, websites reviewed, topic of notes taken, graphics designed, model worked on or built, music recorded, and so on.

Next Time: Write your goals for your next work session or the next step in the project. Include any additional materials or resources needed.

Keep this in your work folder.

Date	Today	Next Time

Spin-Off

Name:_____

General topic: _____

What is your specific topic? _____

What content or key ideas will you include?

_____

_____

_____

_____

How will you share your work?

Project ideas:

Evaluation Checklist

❑ _____

❑ _____

❑ _____

❑ _____

❑ _____

❑ _____

❑ _____

Reading Around the Topic

Name:_____

Topic to be explored:_____

Looking at many resources on your topic is a good way to help you choose a narrower topic for your project. Use this form to keep track of all the resources you view and write down possible subtopics that interest you.

Resources Reviewed

Books (Include title, author, publisher, publisher location, copyright, page numbers reviewed, and where you found the book.)

Magazines/Newspapers/Journals (Include title of resource, volume number, publication date, title and author of article, page numbers, and where you found the resource.)

Websites as well as online resources such as journals and newspapers (Include URL, name of author or organization as appropriate.)

Other resources, such as interviews, software, videos, and museum/art exhibits (Include, as needed, the name of person, title of software or video, or location of exhibit.)

After exploring my topic, I'm interested in the following subtopics: _____

_____

_____

Adapted from *Teaching Gifted Kids in Today's Classroom: Strategies and Techniques Every Teacher Can Use* by Susan Winebrenner with Dina Brulles © 2012. Used with permission from Free Spirit Publishing Inc.

Resources Log

Name:_____

Topic of study:_____

Resources Used

Books (Include title, author, publisher, publisher location, copyright, and page numbers.)

Magazines/Newspapers/Journals (Include title of resource, volume number, publication date, title and author of article, and page numbers.)

Websites as well as online resources such as journals and newspapers (Include URL, name of author or organization as appropriate.)

Other resources, such as interviews, software, videos, and museum/art exhibits (Include, as needed, the name of person, title of software or video, or location of exhibit.)

Project Planner and Checklist

Name:_____

❑ **1. Due date for topic and questions:** _____

The specific topic I will investigate: _____

The specific questions I will investigate (list as many who/what/why/when/where/how questions as appropriate):

_____

_____

❑ **2. Due date for resources:**_____

The resources I will use (minimum of three)

   ❑ Print resources (books, magazines, journals)

   _____

   _____

   ❑ Websites as well as online resources such as journals and newspapers

   _____

   _____

   _____

   ❑ Other resources (interviews, software, videos, exhibits)

   _____

   _____

❑ **3. Due date for product description:** _____

Describe your product: _____

_____

❑ **4. Due date for evaluation checklist:** _____

Evaluation checklist: Complete the checklist to evaluate your project and have a classmate complete one to give you feedback on your project.

❑ **5. Due date for decision about sharing:** _____

I will share my project using

   ❑ a display
   ❑ a presentation

❑ **6. Due date for self-reflection:** _____

Complete the Self-Reflection form.

Self-Reflection

Name:_____

Describe your project:_____

_____

_____

_____

Write four "I learned" statements to describe something new you learned by doing your project.

1. I learned _____

2. I learned _____

3. I learned _____

4. I learned _____

What are two things about your project that you are particularly proud of?

1. _____

2. _____

Describe something you would improve or do differently if you had an opportunity to change something about your project.

What was the most difficult part of this project?

What was the most enjoyable part?

On a scale of 1 to 4 (4 is highest), how would you rate your project?   1   2   3   4

Why do you give it that rating?

CHAPTER 8

What About Grading?

One of the biggest concerns teachers express about differentiated instruction is how to grade assignments and projects fairly when students are engaged in different activities at varied levels of difficulty. To answer the question, you need to consider your philosophy of grading. Consider the following notion: **The primary purpose of grades is to give students (and their parents) feedback about their learning progress and the quality of their work.** Ideally, grading should not compare one student to another, nor should it be used to coerce students into getting their work done. If you have to give grades (and most of us do), grade to help students understand where they are in the learning continuum (beginning, progressing, or at mastery or competency level) and grade the degree to which their performance reflects your criteria for high-quality work.

To make grading fair and equitable, students need to clearly understand your expectations. Each differentiated assignment should have clear evaluation criteria. If students meet the criteria for A work, they get the A. Different tasks or products demand different criteria—a more challenging, complex task will have different criteria than a more basic, foundational task. However, the distinctions between criteria should reflect differences in the *kind* of work students are completing. All tasks—basic or advanced—are evaluated on whether or not they meet the quality criteria *for that task*.

If your students understand that different work has different evaluation criteria; if you have designed your tiered assignments well; and if you take care to make tiering invisible, students and families will consider your grading policies fair.

Establishing Quality Criteria for Differentiated Activities

You need to spell out for students what you'll be looking for in evaluating their work. Your criteria should be:

■ **Clear and concise, yet specific.** Use straightforward language. Clarify vague words like "neat" and "important." What specifically is "neat" work? Not ripped out of a spiral notebook? No crossouts or arrows? Or does it mean legible? What specifically does "important" mean? Key points, concepts, or vocabulary? New developments or perspectives? Reread your criteria after you write them, and ask yourself if students are likely to understand them easily. If not, reexamine the language and ask: How else could I say this?

■ **In kids' language.** Use language that students understand (obviously, this will differ from one age group to the other). Avoid educational jargon. Instead of writing, "Draws comparisons between two political positions," write, "Compares the positions of two groups on the issue." If you're going to share criteria with parents at conferences, in portfolios, or in letters home, it's important that parents understand how you evaluate their children's work. Kids' language will be the best for all concerned.

■ **A reflection of high-level expectations.** Describe high-quality work, not passable work. Instead of "Has fewer than four spelling errors," write, "Uses correct spelling." Criteria shouldn't invite less than the highest-quality work.

■ **Written as positive statements.** Describe what you want, not what you don't want. Instead of "Doesn't clutter poster with too many graphics and text," write, "Uses white space effectively."

■ **Phrased to describe the floor, not the ceiling.** We all know that if we ask students for four examples, we get four examples—no more. State minimum criteria: "Include at least four examples." In this way, you're not setting limits but encouraging effort.

Grades Are Cumulative

Some teachers are concerned that differentiated tasks and the grades assigned to them will affect the calculation of end-of-term grades. How do we avoid sending false messages to students and their parents about their level of achievement in relation to other students in the class? For example, if we grade differentiated tasks based on different evaluation criteria, how do we avoid inflating the grades of students who complete less complex assignments?

Be sure students and parents understand that differentiated tasks are but one consideration in your grading. Final grades reflect not just differentiated activities but also daily work, tests, performance assessments, and assignments required of all students. You have a lot of evidence of student performance to consider. You're also likely to give more weight to certain grades based on their point values; for example, a performance assessment done by all students may be worth 30 points, and a differentiated assignment might be worth 10 or 15 points, depending on its complexity. You control the point value of each letter grade and the degree to which each grade influences the final grade.

You may find it helpful to note in your grade book which grades reflect differentiated tasks. You may even want to note the level of task each grade represents. For example, an A on an advanced task might be noted as "A1." An A on a basic task might be noted as "A2." The code will help you calculate final grades.

Don't Grade Everything

All students need feedback on the quality of their work. However, you don't need to be the only one providing such feedback. **Teach students to assess their own work and to provide and receive peer evaluation, using your criteria for quality work.** Model the use of evaluation checklists if students haven't had much experience using them. Once they understand, they can use your checklists to guide their work and to evaluate their final products. Learning to do self-evaluation and peer evaluation strengthens students' independence and judgment. Such

evaluations also release you from feeling that only you can review student work.

Also, remember that letter grades aren't the only way to provide feedback on student work. Replace them at times with a check, a comment, or a plus or minus sign. Some students' motivation declines when they feel their work doesn't count if it isn't graded. These students are hooked on grades. Try to prevent this by providing meaningful feedback and limiting your use of letter grades.

Peer Evaluation

Peer evaluation isn't likely to be productive or accurate unless you give students evaluation criteria. Without criteria, it becomes nothing more than a popularity contest. Requiring students to use evaluation checklists helps keep peer evaluation fair and free of outside influence. Peers can provide valuable feedback that students can make use of to improve, revise, or redesign a project before it comes to you. For some projects, peer evaluation paired with self-assessment may be sufficient feedback for students. You may simply decide to check in such work.

Grades = Rigor

Some teachers offer assignments to students based on a system of assigning particular grades to particular activities. Fairness becomes an issue when the only difference between an A project and a B project is the amount of work. One way to be sure grades on student-selected projects reflect differences in rigor rather than differences in amount of work is to offer a choice of assignments correlated with their challenge level in Bloom's taxonomy. If students choose to complete an A-level project, they should, in fact, be engaged in more rigorous, challenging work than you deem necessary for a B-level or C-level project. For example:

- To earn a grade of A, the student selects a project at the analyze, evaluate, and/or create levels of challenge.

- To earn a grade of B, the student selects a project at the apply and/or analyze level.

- To earn a grade of C, the student selects a project from the recall, understand, and/or apply level.

Provide evaluation criteria for each project. Clarify for students that they must meet the criteria to earn the designated grade. In other words, choosing an A-level project doesn't automatically result in an A. To earn the A, students must produce work that reflects the evaluation criteria for A work. Otherwise, they may get a lower grade. Those students willing to take on more rigorous work get higher grades. For an example of this type of project, see Figure 23.

This grading strategy is appropriate only when students are given a choice of projects based on the grade they'd like to earn. It is not appropriate for use with tiered assignments assigned to flexible instructional groups; in that case, you'd be limiting students who do excellent work on more basic tasks to lower grades.

Remember that **all students can think and work at higher challenge levels.** All projects should be available to all students. **Keep your criteria for quality work high, yet attainable with effort.** Expect to see different work resulting from the same project. Some students will go much further or be more elaborate in the development of their project. Others will meet the quality criteria but will present a more basic application of the criteria to their work. That's okay! You're encouraging them to take the challenge, recognizing that the end results will look different depending on their interests and capabilities. For students with special needs or individual education plans, you can also modify criteria or requirements as appropriate.

FIGURE 23

Grading Based on Rigor
(appropriate for student-selected projects)

For a Grade of C
Recall/Understand/Apply

- Do a time line or storyboard of events in a news story that was reported over several days.

- Collect all the stories in the main section of your newspaper for three days. Organize the stories from each day into a scrapbook of "Good News" and "Bad News." Count up the number of stories of each kind. Write your conclusions on the final page of your scrapbook.

For a Grade of B
Apply/Analyze

- Collect stories that focus on one gender or the other. Organize them in a scrapbook according to the section of the paper you found them in (for example, sports, business, variety). Examine the number of articles about men and about women and where they appear in the paper. What patterns do you notice? Use graphs or charts to illustrate your points.

- Write a letter to the editor related to a story that you find controversial or that you have strong feelings or beliefs about. Present facts from the published article and provide supporting evidence for your beliefs or position.

For a Grade of A
Analyze/Evaluate/Create

- Design interview questions for a key person in a current news story. Your questions should cover not only important issues and events in the story but also new developments of your own creation. With a classmate, role-play your interview and audio or video record it.

- Examine a current issue in the news and create two editorial cartoons, each presenting a different viewpoint on the issue.

Middle school math teachers in White Bear Lake, Minnesota,* developed the following assessment task. They wanted a way for students to give evidence of their mastery of unit outcomes, but they also wanted to encourage students to stretch beyond basic demonstrations of their math skills. Students' choice of a C-level project provides the necessary evidence of their learning, but choosing B- or A-level work involves them in more complexity, stretches their thinking, and asks them to extend their learning to real-life contexts.

FIGURE 24

Area and Volume Checkup

For this checkup, you can choose the grade you would like to earn.

For a C ➡ You must do questions 1 through 6.

For a B ➡ You must do questions 1 through 9.

For an A ➡ You must do the entire checkup.

To earn the grade at each level, you must do quality work. Quality work shows a strong understanding of the math, uses accurate mathematical strategies, and provides clear explanations.

It is important to understand that you are not guaranteed the grade you are attempting to earn. Choosing your task is just your starting point.

Date due: _____

Name: _____

Part 1

This flat pattern can be folded on the dotted lines to make a box.

1. What will the surface area of the box be? (Remember to label units and show work.)

2. What will the volume of the box be when folded up? (Remember to label units and show work.)

Part 2

Sweet Tooth Chocolates is marketing a special assortment of caramels. They want to put 16 individual caramels in the box. Each caramel is 1 cubic inch.

3. List all the ways that 16 caramels can be neatly packaged in a box.

4. Which arrangement of caramels would require the most cardboard for the box? Why?

5. Which arrangement of caramels would require the least cardboard for the box? Why?

6. On grid paper, draw a flat pattern for the box you described in question 5.

*Thanks to Genni Steele, Nancy Hall, Nadine Cory, Michelle Skorjaniec, and Brenda Sammon.

Part 3

Choose three rectangular product boxes from the bin in our classroom.

7. Find the dimensions of each box. Below, write down the product name and its dimensions.

Product name	Dimensions
1.	
2.	
3.	

8. Find the volume and surface area of each box. *Please show work.*

Box	Volume	Surface Area
1.		
2.		
3.		

9. Is it possible for two boxes to have the same volume but different surface areas? Prove/disprove with an example.

10. Why do you think most products are *not* packaged in the shape that uses the least packaging material? Give real-life examples to support your answer.

11. Choose one of your boxes. Design a box with the same volume but with a smaller surface area than the original. Make sure you give the new dimensions and prove that it has a smaller surface area and the same volume.

Totally 10

You may be concerned that students who take on more complex and challenging projects need more time to complete their activities than do students doing more basic tasks. How do you equalize students' time commitments? Totally 10 is a format for differentiating projects or assessments that may help you better manage such time issues. Students choose activities at different levels of challenge and complexity. Each task they can choose is given a score of 2, 4, 6, or 10. Students must select one project or several that add up to a score of 10. Use the following criteria* for tiering projects, assigning scores, and calculating a final grade:

Score 2

■ Projects at recall, understand, and/or apply level

■ Accounts for 20 percent of final grade

Score 4

■ Projects at apply and/or analyze level

■ Accounts for 40 percent of final grade

Score 6

■ Projects at analyze, evaluate, and/or create level

■ Accounts for 60 percent of final grade

Score 10

■ Projects at analyze, evaluate, and/or create level

■ Exhibits greater complexity, depth, or abstractness than do Score 6 projects

■ A WOW project that reflects rigor rather than simply more work

■ Accounts for 100 percent of final grade

*Adapted from an idea of Laura Magner in "Reaching All Children Through Differentiated Assessment: The 2–5–8 Plan," *Gifted Child Today*, vol. 23, no. 3, May/June 2000, pp. 48–50. Used with permission.

Students can select several smaller projects; for example, one Score 6 project and two Score 2 projects, or one Score 6 and one Score 4 project. Or students could choose the most challenging activity, a Score 10, and do just that one project. Requiring several smaller projects or one or two complex projects should result in students completing work on similar timetables.

Some guidelines for Totally 10:

1. With the exception of a Score 10 project, students must select projects from at least two categories (that is, not everything from Score 2).

2. Projects at each level are graded on quality criteria provided to students ahead of time. Projects must meet quality criteria to be considered A work and receive full points.

3. Final grades are calculated from a weighted perspective. For example, earning an A on a Score 2 project (20 percent) does not have the weight of earning an A on a Score 6 project (60 percent). All projects are important, however, since they contribute to a cumulative final grade.

The following figure shows Totally 10 projects for a unit on mythology.

FIGURE 25

Totally 10 Projects: Mythology

Score 2 (20 percent of final grade)

- Construct a family tree of Greek gods, goddesses, mortals, and creatures.

- Illustrate a poster showing corresponding Greek and Roman gods and goddesses.

- Present an adventure of a god, goddess, or creature through storytelling.

Score 4 (40 percent of final grade)

- Make a chart comparing and contrasting a mythical character from another culture to a Greek or Roman mythical character.

- Identify a contemporary superhero with characteristics of heroes from mythology. Write a newspaper article describing how this hero has mythical traits.

Score 6 (60 percent of final grade)

- Script an original dialogue between two mythical characters. Include accurate and complete information about their characteristics and adventures.

- Design an illustrated mystery booklet of mythical characters called "Who Am I?" Include adventures as well as personal and family details as clues.

- Create a rap, jingle, or song to help people remember the names of mythical characters, their characteristics, and one of their adventures.

Totally 10 (100 percent of final grade)

- Create a mythical character for our 21st century. Write a character sketch to identify your character's personality, physical appearance, and powers. Dramatize, do storytelling, make a video, or create an action comic book of an original adventure. Include appropriate elements of mythological tales.

CHAPTER 9

How Do You Manage Differentiation?

Managing a differentiated classroom really involves three issues: How do I prepare to differentiate? How do I prepare my students and my classroom? How do I manage the groups and activities? You've read management tips throughout this book as they applied to various strategies. This chapter will summarize those tips and provide some additional thoughts and ideas.

Preparing to Differentiate

Learning new teaching strategies can feel overwhelming. But remember: no one expects you to differentiate your entire curriculum overnight—or even in a single school year. Teaching isn't magic. It's hard work. It takes planning, time, and a great deal of energy. You're on your way to a more learner-responsive classroom the moment you take the risk of trying one of the strategies in this book. You haven't failed if a strategy doesn't work for you—you've succeeded when you adapt it or decide to try a different one.

Start Small

■ Try one new idea or strategy at a time. Once you feel confident using it, try another.

■ Select one curricular area or one unit to differentiate—not your whole curriculum.

Start with What Is

■ Acknowledge what you already do. Do you pretest? Do you individualize any part of your curriculum? Do you sometimes allow students to skip ahead or stay with a topic longer? Have you made the commitment to know your students and to make learning relevant to them?

■ Use the lenses of challenge and variety to determine how differentiated your current units are. Acknowledge (and celebrate!) what you already have and examine what's missing.

■ Get ideas for tiered assignments from your teacher's editions, your current curriculum, and your peers.

■ Sort your existing activities. Which should all students do? Which are only appropriate for some? Which could be eliminated altogether?

■ Assign existing activities with the principles of differentiation in mind. Ask, "Which students would benefit most from this?"

Preparing Your Students and Classroom

■ Talk with students about the fact that we all learn differently. Help them understand that assignments don't have to be the same to be fair.

■ Use brief, tiered activities from project menus or challenge centers as warm-ups or cool-downs. This approach will help students get used to handling tiered activities. Ask the whole class to do them first. Then use them as you work with flexible groups.

■ Develop your students' skills of independence in whole-group activities. Then help them apply the skills to small-group work, partner work, and individual work.

■ Set up behavior guidelines, post them, discuss them, and be consistent about enforcing them.

■ Discuss expected behavior for collaborative work: stay on task, participate, listen carefully, share ideas, and support each other's contributions.

■ Provide guidelines for sound levels during work time. How much noise is allowable? Give students metaphors such as, "Use eight-inch voices. No one farther away should be able to hear your voice."

■ Develop a signal for quiet. Raise a hand as your cue for students to both stop talking and raise their own hands. Ring a chime or bell. You need an established way to get their attention when you're providing directions or moving groups.

■ Arrange your classroom for group work. Put materials or supplies at workstations to limit the need for students to move around to get what they need.

■ Establish routines for distributing student folders, getting and returning supplies, and turning in completed work. Select students to deliver and pick up necessary materials.

■ Set up patterns for movement around the room. How will students break into groups? Discuss procedures and, as appropriate, practice them before they are used.

■ Establish routines so students know what to do when they finish a task early.

■ Set clear guidelines about your availability during flexible group time. One teacher puts a ponytail scrunchy on her right wrist when she wants to signal "Not now." Another hangs a red card on a lanyard he wears around his neck. When the lanyard is on, he is not available for questions, he's teaching. You may wish to devise a cue that students can use to get your assistance when you are available. This avoids having them sit passively with their hands raised. Try providing a red card to be placed in a corner of a desk when your assistance is needed. When you're available, look for the red cards. Systems like these are crucial to helping your class run smoothly.

Think Through the Task in Advance

■ How will I distribute materials?

■ How will I give directions?

■ What level of noise is appropriate for this activity?

■ What movement will be necessary around the classroom?

■ What is the best arrangement for the classroom?

■ How and when can students get my assistance?

■ How will I use my time?

■ When and where can I best meet with each group?

■ What are students to do when they finish an activity early?

Consider What Can Be Done Ahead of Time

■ Divide group materials into plastic bags or bins.

■ Have group assignments and workcards ready to go.

■ Arrange work folders.

■ Have a place for students to store work.

■ Have cool-down activities ready in case a lesson doesn't last as long as you planned or if students finish early.

Don't Forget the Families

■ Keep families informed with newsletters, notes, and emails, as appropriate.

■ Take the time to answer questions and concerns that families may have about differentiation. Listen thoughtfully and then explain *specifically* how a differentiated classroom will meet their child's needs.

■ Get family members involved as volunteers during flexible group time or seek their help at home in doing such tasks as laminating workcards with contact paper.

Managing Student Work

Who Goes Where?

■ At the beginning of group time, post names on the board or a flip chart to let students know which group they're in.

■ Organize name cards into work groups on a pocket chart.

- If you're using challenge centers for tiered assignments (see Chapter 7, pages 113–115), try this idea suggested by a classroom teacher: Assign particular centers to students by using colored tickets. Code the centers by color so you'll know which are more basic or foundational and which are advanced or more challenging (for example, red and orange tickets for basic centers, blue and green tickets for advanced centers). Place students' name cards down the left column of a pocket chart. Behind each name, tuck colored tickets for the centers most appropriate for each student. As students complete their station, they move their ticket from behind their name to the column across from their name on the pocket chart. This allows you to simply glance at the chart and see each student's progress. Laminate your tickets so you can use them over and over. Remember to vary the colors—you don't want blue tickets to always indicate advanced centers.

- Before students arrive, list the names of each group's members on a table tent (a large sheet of paper folded three times will stand up well). Students find their group and work area by looking for their name on a table tent. You could also have students take their regularly assigned seats and then read each group's names as you place a tent in an assigned work area.

- You can also designate each work area by a color or number on a table tent. On the board or a flip chart, list student names by group and note each group's designated color or number. Students find their names, determine the color or number assigned to their group, and proceed to their designated work area.

How Do You Set Things Up?

- You can use plastic bins or tubs to organize materials and workcards. Everything students need for the task goes in the container. Include a checklist for restocking supplies after students have finished working.

- Have hanging file folders for each student, where they can retrieve their work and store unfinished assignments. Use the files to drop in work for students who are absent. Organize files by the hour or period of the day.

- If you don't have counters to use for distributing materials, ask your custodian for extra desks that you could push together to make a distribution center.

- Use stacking letter files to hold supplies and for submitting completed work. Secondary teachers may wish to label these by hour or section to eliminate the need to sort papers.

- Staple open pocket folders to your bulletin board to hold reference materials, directions, or worksheets. Color code or number them to correlate each item with a task (for example, red task materials are in the red folder, task 1 materials are in folder 1).

- Ask one student from each group to distribute supplies and materials.

- Position yourself and your groups so you can see them at all times.

- Provide storage room for larger, bulkier projects in progress. Use a back counter, a table, or plastic crates.

How Do You Manage Directions?

- Use workcards to provide step-by-step directions for individual, partner, or group tasks. As needed, include a checklist of quality criteria on the workcard. For frequent use, laminate the cards or slide them into clear page protectors.

- Set up workstations to organize materials and resources. Use a nearby bulletin board to post directions and work samples, as appropriate. Create a work area by using a trifold poster board with mounted pockets to hold directions and paper resources or supplies. Keep the poster board generic in its design so you can continue to use it when your curriculum topic changes.

- Provide procedure checklists for each task. Students can use them to check off steps or components as each is completed.

■ Give directions both orally and visually. Keep written directions available (on work-cards, a flip chart, or the board, or by other means) for students to refer back to. Audio record directions and place them at workstations. Parent volunteers could do this if you provide the script.

■ Choose a student in each group to be a teacher's aide. Give aides directions for tasks before the work session begins and have them give the directions to the group. Aides can also collect questions from group members, answer questions, or resolve confusions for members of their group. Be sure every student has a chance to be an aide at one time or another.

■ Use study buddies. Pair a student who has difficulty with directions or follow-through with another student in the group. The buddy presents or explains the directions and answers questions.

How Do You and Your Students Keep Track of Work?

You keep track

■ Through observations and informal chats with students at work.

■ Through checklists on clipboards or comments on notecards or self-stick notes that are later placed in student files.

■ Through scheduled conferences with students.

■ By posting "office hours" that say when you are available to talk with students about their work.

■ By reviewing student self-evaluations using checklists of quality criteria.

■ By skimming through student work and worklogs, found in each student's hanging file folder.

Students keep track through

■ Worklogs (see page 118) on which they record their progress on an activity that spans several class periods.

■ Procedure checklists that ask them to check off each component of a project or activity as it is completed.

■ Checklists of quality criteria that guide their work and encourage self-evaluation.

■ Peer reviews. Students meet with a partner from their work group. Using your checklist of quality criteria, students review each other's work and provide feedback. Ask partners to sign the checklist so they'll feel accountable for a careful review. Using a whiteboard or an example copy, demonstrate the process of peer evaluation so students can see how it works.

■ Time lines and checkpoints, which encourage them to keep on track with longer-term activities. Set due dates for submission of components or of completed work.

Making your classroom organized and flexible enough to provide sufficient structure for individual work yet be "small-group friendly" is important. This does not mean that your room has to be the neatest classroom in your school, just one that supports the organization and movement of materials and students within its walls. Establishing clear procedures and practices in your classroom will provide your students a greater opportunity to work independently and lessen your need to monitor student behavior and "direct traffic." Together, both will put you clearly on the road to success in a differentiated classroom.

CHAPTER 10

How Do You Differentiate for Special Populations?

In the preceding chapters, we looked at differentiating instruction based on factors such as aptitude, readiness, learning pace, interests, learning styles, and learning preferences. There are, however, two other important aspects of student diversity: the special learning needs of gifted and talented students and of students with various learning disabilities (or learning differences). The particular learning profiles of these populations demand different kinds of differentiation. It's beyond the scope of this book to provide a comprehensive guide to differentiating for special populations, but the following perspectives may help you examine the basics of differentiation for these students. Creating a better instructional match in the classroom has benefits for *all* students.

Differentiated Instruction and Special Needs Students

Students who have an IEP (individualized education program) or a 504 plan (for students with special needs who don't qualify for special education services) can benefit from differentiated instruction as long as you make modifications based on their specific learning needs. Use the information and recommendations presented in the IEP or 504 plan to guide you. Place students with special needs in flexible instructional groups as appropriate. In inclusive classrooms, there may be benefits to scheduling flexible groups when an aide or paraprofessional is available to help with management. If you're using project menus and challenge center activities with all students, keep the needs of special education learners in mind. **You don't need to develop separate tiered assignments for these students; instead, modify the tasks to make them more appropriate.** Work closely with special education colleagues to determine the appropriateness of differentiated tasks for particular students.

Like all learners, students with special needs are unique individuals with distinct learning preferences and interests. The following general descriptions of special-needs students may describe specific students you work with.

Response to Intervention

The 2004 reauthorization of Individuals with Disabilities Education Act (IDEA) prompted schools to move away from a discrepancy model, which relied on intelligence test scores and classroom performance, to determine the presence of a learning disability. RTI, or Response to Intervention (in some states called Response to Instruction), is the new paradigm in considering the needs of students who may exhibit learning difficulties.

Teachers as part of a team identify a student's academic difficulties; determine the student's strengths, interests, and talents; review data on the student's learning progress; and design specific interventions to increase the likelihood of the student's success in learning. The critical elements of differentiation are the very foundation of RTI. Teachers are not able to effectively design specific student interventions without knowledge of and instructional strategies for differentiation.

RTI is typically presented as a three-stage model.

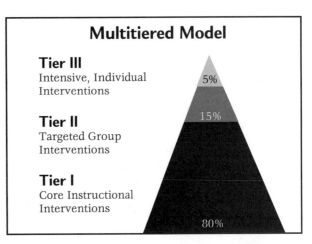

Multitiered Model

Tier III
Intensive, Individual
Interventions

5%

Tier II
Targeted Group
Interventions

15%

Tier I
Core Instructional
Interventions

80%

Tier I

In Tier I, all students are engaged in differentiated instruction in the general curriculum. Baseline data is collected on students who are having difficulties academically. Classroom teachers may design more specific interventions for these students and must monitor their progress. If instruction is appropriately differentiated using research-based best practices, RTI proponents assert that 80 to 90 percent of students will be successful in learning.

Tier II

If students do not make adequate progress in Tier I, more intensive interventions are implemented. Tier II strategies include the use of small groups and more intensive instruction that is reflective of flexible instructional groups and tiered assignments used in differentiation. Progress continues to be monitored and instruction adjusted as appropriate. RTI proponents suggest that an additional 5 to 10 percent of students can be successful with the help of the Tier II strategies.

Tier III

When students do not adequately respond to the Tier II interventions, the special education referral and due process procedures may be initiated. The school obtains parental consent and begins evaluation procedures for the student. All information available on the student from Tier I and II interventions, as well as from additional assessment related to cognitive, achievement, and adaptive behavior functioning, is reviewed. An individual educational plan may result. It is suggested that no more than 5 percent of students should need Tier III interventions.

It is assumed that most students can succeed in learning if instruction is appropriately differentiated using research-based best practices.

Learning differences may include limitations in listening, thinking, speaking, reading, writing, spelling, or doing math. Such students may have difficulty processing visual or auditory information. In differentiating their instruction, you need to consider these specific obstacles.

Students with visual processing difficulties have trouble with information taken in through the eyes. Examples include differentiating form, shape, pattern, size, or position and perceiving spatial or whole/part relationships. These difficulties may interfere with a student's ability to accurately identify numbers and letters, gain information from charts and graphs, or use other information presented visually. What does this mean for differentiation? For some students, it means limiting or modifying activities that present material in visual/spatial and, to some degree, verbal/linguistic ways. You can also help students by allowing them to show what they've learned in ways other than these.

Students with auditory processing difficulties usually experience challenges in analyzing and making sense of information presented orally. They may also have trouble hearing differences in sounds or in reconstructing sounds into syllables and words. They typically take longer to process what they hear. For instance, it may be difficult for them to follow verbal directions. Not only are students' speech and language influenced, but also their ability to read and spell. This means that if you rely heavily on verbal/linguistic presentations of new concepts and skills, you may hinder their learning. Consider modifying your requirements for verbal/linguistic projects and assessments. Allow these students to show what they've learned in other ways.

When the achievement level of a student with learning differences varies considerably from that of other students in a class, you'll need to work with special education colleagues to determine the best ways to differentiate instruction for that student. You'll want to carefully examine the student's specific learning patterns. For example, if the student is reading significantly below grade level, differentiation may include providing reading materials at the appropriate level or designing study guides to help the student read and comprehend textbooks.

Much of what is presented in school relies on sight or sound. For students with learning differences, some classrooms are "worlds of words" they cannot easily process. Do all students need reading, writing, speaking, and listening skills? Yes. But you can help students with learning differences succeed by offering them variety in processes and products while maintaining appropriate levels of challenge. **Differentiation is the best instructional response for all students, including those with learning differences.**

Behavior Disorders

Although students with behavior disorders such as EBD (emotional or behavioral disorders), ADD (attention deficit disorder), or ODD (oppositional defiant disorder) are sometimes discussed together, they can have very different needs. Behavior disorders typically affect students' ability to pay attention, get along with others, and follow directions. Hyperactivity, distractibility, and impulsivity may interfere with their learning and their social interactions within the classroom.

To motivate students with behavior disorders, design differentiated activities based on their specific learning needs, strengths, and interests. When you're planning activities, pay special attention to management issues. For example, provide highly structured activities and supply checklists of procedures or steps to follow. Develop routines for helping students manage behavior and work. Plan time to guide and encourage students, and build in appropriate opportunities for them to move about the room. For these students in particular, you may want to use flexible instructional groups on days when you have paraprofessionals or aides in the classroom to assist you with management.

Physical Disabilities/Differences

Physical disabilities may affect students' mobility but not their need for differentiated instruction. Work with your special education colleagues as appropriate in modifying tasks such as bodily/kinesthetic activities. Keep physical restrictions in mind as you plan lessons, field trips, and events. Work to arrange your classroom so students with physical differences can participate fully.

Autism Spectrum Disorders

Autism spectrum disorders include PDD (pervasive development disorder), autism, and Asperger syndrome (normal intelligence and language development but with autistic-like behaviors and deficiencies in social and communication skills). Students with such disorders may be very high functioning—even gifted and talented—or they may require extensive support from special education services. They typically have problems with social interaction and may exhibit repetitive behavior patterns or unusual obsessions. They may have motor deficits, difficulty taking turns, a lack of judgment, and highly uneven academic skills.

As you would with students who have behavior disorders, pay special attention to management issues when differentiating activities. In managing routines and interacting with others, students with autism spectrum disorders often benefit through the use of visual cues, such as icons or pictograms. **As with all your students, give lots of opportunities to work independently on activities that reflect their learning preferences and current interests.**

Dual Differences

Some students are "twice exceptional," requiring both special education and gifted education services. For example, researchers and educators have recently begun exploring giftedness in some children with Asperger syndrome. As you differentiate instruction for students with learning differences, try to be attuned to learning needs that may be masked by their disorder. **Take care not to focus solely on the disability.** Sometimes a gift may be hidden or unrecognized because of a student's behavioral or learning difficulties.

Meet with your special education colleagues to review the student's IEP file. What evidence can you find of the student's cognitive abilities? What differentiation strategies can best address the student's needs? Make sure the IEP details plans for the student's intellectual stimulation and academic growth, as well as for the learning difficulties.

An Idea from Your Special Education Colleagues

To identify the best ways for your special education students to learn and to present what they have learned, use Gardner's multiple intelligences. If you're a classroom teacher, sit down with your special education colleagues and discuss your students with them, referring to these guidelines. If you're a special education teacher, use the following guidelines to create a differentiation profile for your students.

For each student with special needs:

1. Review strengths, abilities, disabilities, and special education concerns.

2. Think about your perceptions of the student's learning preferences.

3. Identify any special considerations needed for this student, such as management of learning activities, adjustments for behavioral issues, and modified classroom arrangements.

4. Using a Gardner product list (such as the ones in Projects, Presentations, Performances on pages 34–38), identify:

   ■ Projects that the student could complete independently.

   ■ Projects that the student could complete independently with some modifications.

   ■ Projects that the student could do in a group with other classmates.

   ■ Projects that the student could do with a paraprofessional or aide.

5. Consider specific modifications of particular projects. For example, ask the student to record a conversation between two characters in a book rather than write out the conversation.

This process and the information it provides will help you differentiate learning activities and projects to best address the needs of your special education students. Your special education colleagues may benefit, too. By working with you

on differentiation concerns, they may develop new ideas on making classroom activities more responsive to students' learning preferences, strengths, and interests.

Other Differentiation Strategies for Special Needs Students

Here are some additional tips for differentiating instruction for students with special needs. Of course, these strategies could also be helpful to other learners in your classroom.

■ Use paired or group reading as necessary and appropriate.

■ Present directions in more than one way: orally, and then on procedure checklists, flip charts, or enable the students to see the actual work page using a document camera.

■ Use procedure checklists to help students remember what to do and in what order. Remind them to check off each step as it is completed.

■ Provide a variety of ways for students to learn new material (for example, mini-lectures, digital audio recorders, video, print or online materials, iPad applications).

■ Assign "study buddies" to help with directions as necessary.

■ Use a digital audio recorder to record directions so students can refer to them as needed.

■ Respect the need of some students to move around. Identify and clearly communicate when students may leave their work places and where they can go.

■ Provide a stopwatch to remind your more kinetic students of when they can move about. Set the watch for the amount of time you consider appropriate for the student to stay on task. When they reach that time, they may get up and move.

■ Provide a quiet, attractive space for students who learn or work best away from others.

- For learners with visual difficulties, read aloud written information, directions, and procedures.

- For learners with auditory difficulties, provide maps, charts, lists, or icons to move them through tasks. Provide work samples to help them see the quality of work you expect.

- Think about the physical arrangement of your classroom. Are there active and quiet areas? Is the seating arrangement conducive to the needs of all students? Are rows, clusters, or semicircles best?

- Consider allowing students to use headphones (without a player or radio attached) to block noise and distractions.

All students have areas of strength, expertise, and interest, and differentiating instruction will help provide variety and challenge for both regular education and special education students.

Differentiated Instruction for Gifted and Talented Students

Gifted students have specific learning differences that call for specific differentiation techniques. Simply increasing challenge and variety may not be enough. Here are some typical characteristics that gifted learners exhibit:

1. High levels of retention with an extraordinary amount of information. Some gifted students become specialists in a topic or subject area at a young age. Intellectual curiosity motivates them to absorb everything they can about the topics they are passionate about. These learners also retain information more readily and longer than do their classmates.

2. An accelerated pace of learning. Gifted students don't require the same amount of time and practice as their classmates do to learn something new. In many cases, they already know what you're teaching.

3. Advanced comprehension, deep understanding. Gifted and talented learners not only know facts, but can readily use them. Their intricate understanding and ability to make connections across content areas may far exceed classmates and even some teachers. They tend not to go through the same steps as their peers in understanding things—some simply "leap" to understanding. For this reason, it can be difficult for them to be peer tutors. They may be puzzled when others don't understand what is obvious to them.

4. Unusually varied interests and curiosity. Many gifted students know a lot about a lot. Since they tend to know more than their classmates about particular topics, they may seek out adults as sources of information and conversation. Their curiosity drives them to ask "why" questions and to demand in-depth, specific information.

5. An advanced vocabulary. Because of their curiosity and ability to pursue and retain information, gifted learners often develop a specialized vocabulary particular to their passions.

6. Flexibility in thinking; will approach a task in different ways. Gifted students typically are the ones who will ask if they can do an assignment in another way. They love to be given choices. They will also approach an assignment in ways you may not expect. They may have a tendency to make projects bigger and more time-consuming.

7. An ability to generate original ideas and solutions. Not all gifted learners are especially creative; however, their knowledge base enables many of them to out-think classmates. Creatively gifted students are the ones who push the envelope, taking projects and discussions in new and unexpected directions.

8. An ability to think in abstract terms and sense consequences. Gifted students are able to think abstractly at a younger age than average learners and are comfortable with ambiguities. They are particularly skilled at thinking about cause and effect and potential consequences.

9. Evaluative, judgmental thinking. Gifted learners generally are good critical thinkers and so are quick to identify misinformation, lack of logic, and unclear thinking. They may be quick to note such flaws in others. However, they are also hard on themselves. Shortfalls in performance, even minor ones, may send their self-esteem plummeting.

10. Persistent goal-directed behavior. Although there certainly are gifted learners who underachieve academically, many are able to set personal and academic goals and work efficiently and persistently toward them.

High Achievers vs. Gifted Learners

Not all high-achieving students are gifted. Not all gifted students are high achievers. To appropriately differentiate instruction for gifted learners,

it's important to understand this distinction. Giftedness reflects innate, advanced aptitudes that may or may not emerge as exceptional academic talent over time. In other words, you can be gifted but not talented. High-achieving students know what it takes to be successful in school and are willing to put in the time and effort. Those students who are gifted underachievers may be unable to achieve academic goals because of learning differences or difficulties. They may also be unwilling to commit the time and effort necessary for school success. The following figure will help you make some distinctions between the learning patterns of high achievers and gifted students. Keep in mind that each student is an individual and that few students are likely to be gifted in all the ways listed.

F I G U R E   2 6

A High Achiever vs. A Gifted Learner

A High Achiever	A Gifted Learner
■ Knows the answers	■ Asks the questions
■ Is interested	■ Is highly curious
■ Is attentive	■ Is intellectually engaged
■ Has good ideas	■ Has original ideas
■ Works hard	■ Performs with ease
■ Commits time and effort to learning	■ May need less time to excel
■ Answers questions	■ Responds with detail and unique perspectives
■ Absorbs information	■ Manipulates information
■ Copies and responds accurately	■ Creates new and original products
■ Is a top student	■ Is beyond her or his age peers
■ Needs 6 to 8 repetitions for mastery	■ Needs 1 to 2 repetitions for mastery
■ Understands ideas	■ Constructs abstractions
■ Grasps meaning	■ Draws inferences
■ Completes assignments	■ Initiates projects
■ Is a technician	■ Is an innovator
■ Is a good memorizer	■ Is insightful; makes connections with ease
■ Is receptive	■ Is intense
■ Listens with interest	■ Shows strong feelings, opinions, perspectives
■ Prefers sequential presentation of information	■ Thrives on complexity
■ Is pleased with his or her own learning	■ Is highly self-critical

Based on a concept from "The Gifted and Talented Child" by Janice Szabos, Maryland Council for Gifted & Talented, Inc.

Meet with Colleagues, Examine Your Curriculum

As suggested for special education students, it's a good idea to meet with your school's gifted education teacher or specialist to discuss the specific learning needs of your gifted students. Become aware of the way your school identifies gifted and talented learners. Review the available information to help you understand the learning strengths of gifted students. Find out what resources, training, or materials might be available to you. Even if your school lacks gifted education services, the following information can help you differentiate instruction appropriately for gifted learners.

Spin-offs (see Chapter 7, pages 115–117) provide students an opportunity to explore an area of interest to them. However, the choices you offer may be limited by curriculum requirements. The interests and passions of gifted learners often lie beyond or outside the general curriculum. Instructional looping (see pages 107–111) will help you accommodate differences in skill mastery, but some gifted students are considerably out of alignment with their grade-level curriculum. How do you respond when the issue becomes not what you'll do for gifted students today or this week, but what you'll do for them during an entire unit or grading period? Some answers from the field of gifted education are curriculum compacting, individual planning, and the assistance of mentors or subject area specialists.

But before tackling these three approaches, you might begin your process of differentiation simply by examining your curriculum with the following set of questions in mind (developed using Robert Eberle's creative thinking checklist, SCAMPER). SCAMPER techniques alone do not comprehensively differentiate for gifted learners, but they do prompt your thinking about approaches most appropriate for these learners.

FIGURE 27

Differentiation "SCAMPER"
For Gifted and Talented Students

Substitute
What basic content could I replace with more abstract, advanced, or sophisticated content?

Combine
How can I combine learning with creative thinking to encourage originality and innovation?

Adapt
How can I adapt curriculum to accelerate the pace of instruction?

How can I adapt activities to elicit high levels of performance?

Modify
How can I modify learning to provide greater depth and complexity?

Put to other use
How can I accelerate the pace of instruction so class time can be used for in-depth or advanced learning reflecting students' specific interests and talents?

Eliminate
What mastered content or skills can I eliminate so students can focus on more advanced learning?

Reverse/Rearrange
How can I rearrange or reorganize curriculum to give students time to develop original ideas and products?

Adapted from *Scamper* by Robert Eberle (Waco, TX: Prufrock Press, 1971). Used with permission.

Curriculum Compacting

Compacting* is an essential element in differentiating for gifted and talented students whose content knowledge or skill development is substantially different from their classmates' and who have a strong desire to pursue an interest-based, advanced project. **When you compact curriculum, you examine a particular**

---

*As advocated and described by Sally Reis, Joseph Renzulli, and Deborah Burns in *Curriculum Compacting: The Complete Guide for Modifying the Regular Curriculum for High Ability Students* (Mansfield Center, CT: Creative Learning Press, 1992).

subject area and identify content or skills that could be accelerated, eliminated, or preassessed. You replace your standard coursework with an advanced, interest-based project that students work on during class time. Likely candidates for compacting are students who already have extensive knowledge of a curriculum topic, have mastered a significant number of the skills you're planning to present, or are capable of accelerated learning.

Compacting may have one or more of the following purposes:

■ To eliminate repetition of mastered content and/or skills.

■ To increase the challenge level of the regular curriculum.

■ To provide time for the investigation of a curricular topic that is beyond the scope of the regular curriculum.

As with all differentiation, the first step in compacting is to examine your curriculum and instruction in light of students' needs. Take a look at the curriculum map you began in Chapter 3 (page 70). In addition to using an asterisk to note exit points for differentiation, you can mark items appropriate for curriculum compacting. Use a plus sign (+) for "extend, enrich" and a minus sign (-) for "eliminate, preassess, speed up."

Review the skills and the projects/products sections of your map. Which have you coded at Bloom's lower levels of challenge (recall, understand, apply)? These might be logical ones to compact for gifted students and to replace with more advanced work. Mark these with a minus sign. What content or topics could you extend, enrich, or present in greater depth? Is there advanced content you'd like to introduce? Mark these with a plus sign. These become potential ideas for differentiated projects.

Remember that the projects your gifted students engage in through compacting must be based on interests as well as complexity. Collaborate with students to determine the content and topic of the project, the way the work will be accomplished, and the way the results

will be shared. **As with most students, but particularly with gifted learners, the key to motivation is interest.** If students are interested in and dedicated to a project, they are more likely to follow through with it.

Remember, too, that the projects or investigations that are developed through compacting must be above and beyond the interests and capabilities of average learners. If most students could do such a project, then the project does not reflect sufficient rigor to warrant a gifted student's release from general curriculum requirements. Keep the criteria for challenge clearly in mind as you plan "instead of" learning for your gifted students: differentiation for gifted students must reflect a distinctively different level of challenge. The following figure presents these special aspects of challenge.

FIGURE   28

Aspects of Challenge for Gifted Students

■ Original thinking

■ Working with concepts and generalizations rather than strictly factual knowledge

■ Complex thinking

■ Readiness for learning based on the student, rather than on the grade/age level

■ Accelerated pace of learning

■ Advanced, sophisticated content

■ Abstract concepts

■ Interdisciplinary work

■ Critical evaluation

■ Problem seeking and problem solving

■ Innovation

■ Capitalizing on advanced interests and curiosity

■ Actively involving student in planning and decisions

■ Feedback from experts

Page 144 has an example of a compacting form you might use with your gifted students. (For a blank form you can use, see page 146.) Notice the spaces for the signatures of student, teacher, and parent. Curriculum compacting is a collaborative effort between student and teacher. Also, as with any special learning plan, it's helpful to involve and inform the student's family. You want the family to share your commitment to differentiating this gifted student's learning. After you and the student have developed the plan, you might schedule a parent conference or talk to a family member by telephone or via email. Ask a parent or guardian to sign the compacting form, indicating their agreement and support for the project.

In the left column of the form, identify the curricular area you'll be compacting, based on the student's academic strengths. For the student in the example, fifth-grader Libby Clark, that area is language arts. In the second column, describe what you will speed up, allow the student to test out of, or eliminate. Also describe any responsibilities the student will have toward the regular curriculum. For example, will the student participate in certain class discussions, simulations, or science labs? Will there be particular assignments that the student will be required to complete? In the sample, the teacher has decided to pretest Libby on spelling words and to eliminate spelling practice activities. In the third column, describe the project the student will do instead of typical course requirements. In the sample plan, Libby will create an illustrated collection of her own poetry. Since compacting projects are developed based on student interests, the project described in the third column may or may not be in the same curricular area as the area being compacted.

You and the student need to determine what resources will be needed and what the steps of the project will be. As with all projects, the student needs a checklist of quality criteria to help guide her work and to facilitate self-evaluation when she's finished. Establish a due date for the final project.

Set up a conference schedule so you (or another project advisor, such as a mentor) and the student can discuss the progress of the project, identify any additional resources needed, and make any necessary changes in the plan. Such conferences also give you the chance to provide feedback. Use the Conference Log form on page 147 to record what was discussed and planned.

Several of the forms offered in earlier chapters can be used to manage student projects that result from compacting. To help both you and the student keep track of daily work, use the Worklog, page 118. Depending on the project, you might use Reading Around the Topic, page 120, so the student can explore and narrow down a topic, and Resources Log, page 121, so the student can record actual resources used. Use or adapt the Project Planner and Checklist, page 122, to create a time line for completion of various components of the project. Following the project, you might ask the student to fill out the Self-Reflection on page 123.

Individual Planning

You may, at times, have highly gifted students in your classroom—students whose skills and knowledge far surpass those of their classmates. Although strategies for differentiation lift the general level of instruction in the classroom, this may not be enough for such students, for whom the most advanced tiered assignment is still not a stretch. For them, even being compacted out of a unit or two is insufficient. You are dealing with a year-long curriculum mismatch. Sometimes a student may have a single talent "spike," such as an extraordinary ability in math, or there may be several curriculum areas that offer the student little new learning.

With these students, the most appropriate avenue for differentiating instruction is an individual learning plan. Such a plan must delineate which learning goals or standards have already been met, which still need to be addressed, and how the student will move through the school's curriculum at an appropriate pace and in sufficient depth. Sometimes the plan may advise that the student skip a grade or course, or it may permit the student to attend classes with students in higher grades.

F I G U R E   2 9

Sample: Compacting Form and Project Description*

Name of Student: Libby Clark _____

Signature of Student: _____

Signature of Teacher: _____

Signature of Parent/Guardian: _____

Curriculum Area(s)	Speed up/Test-out/Eliminate	Project Description
Language Arts	Pretest spelling words Eliminate appropriate spelling practice activities	Illustrated poetry

Resources Needed
computer, art paper, watercolors, bookmaking materials and equipment

Steps in the Project

1. Write at least 10 poems in various genres.

2. Illustrate each poem with a watercolor painting.

3. Plan a layout for each page of the poetry collection.

4. Mount each poem and illustration on background paper.

5. Design and construct a cover, title page, and author dedication.

6. Bind the book.

Criteria for Quality Work

____ includes at least 10 poems in various genres

____ presents a watercolor illustration for each poem

____ plans an effective page layout

____ effectively mounts each poem and illustration

____ designs and completes a cover, title page, and author dedication that reflect the content of the book

____ binds the book in a neat and durable manner

Due Date: end of first trimester

*Adapted from *The Compactor* by Joseph S. Renzulli and Linda H. Smith (Mansfield Center, CT: Creative Learning Press, Inc., 1978). Used with permission.

The key to a successfully differentiated learning plan for a gifted student is personalization. Teachers, parents, and student make decisions together about how the student will continue to progress in learning. The top priorities are the learning needs and best interests of the student. It's particularly important that the student be involved in the development of the plan. The student's interest and commitment are critical to its success.

The Importance of Mentors

Teachers of gifted and talented students have traditionally sought mentors and subject area specialists who will provide opportunities for students to go beyond what the curriculum, one teacher, or the school's learning environment can offer. As a classroom teacher who differentiates instruction, you too can **solicit community people or school staff who are willing to work with your gifted students.** Whether a mentor is asked to advance a student's knowledge or skills, provide expert feedback on a product or project, show "real world" use of a student's interests, or simply answer questions for an inquisitive gifted learner, mentorships are often essential for effective differentiation.

Look for mentors and subject area specialists within your own school and community. Some of your teaching colleagues may have hobbies or interests that are shared by one of your advanced students. Do you know someone who's good at photography or at filming and editing their own video productions? How about asking that person to assist the next time a student wants to produce an original video or do a photo essay? Is there someone in another department or grade level who would be willing to provide advanced content or skills to one of your students? Is there a professional in your community who might agree to mentor an interested student or serve as advisor on a project?

At the beginning of the school year, send a mentor recruitment form (such as the one provided on page 148 of this chapter) to staff members, parents, and community members and begin to assemble your own database of experts. Some school districts have volunteers who maintain a bank of community resources. Other districts have created a community resource pool as part of their school's community education program.

Differentiation means responding to students' particular learning needs. Today's classrooms usually include some students with needs related to learning difficulties and some students who are gifted or talented. It's important to include proven differentiation strategies for these populations in your teaching repertoire.

Compacting Form and Project Description

Name of student: _____

Signature of student: _____

Signature of teacher: _____

Signature of parent/guardian: _____

Curriculum Area(s)	Speed up/Test-out/Eliminate	Project Description

Resources needed:

Steps in the project:

Criteria for quality work:

Due date:

Adapted from *The Compactor* by Joseph S. Renzulli and Linda H. Smith (Mansfield Center, CT: Creative Learning Press, 1978). Used with permission.

Conference Log

Name: _____

Project advisor: _____

Topic for the project: _____

Date	Advisor's comments	Goals for next conference	Date of next conference

Mentor and Subject Area Specialist Application

Name: _____

Address: _____

_____

Telephone: _____

Email: _____

What is the best way and time to reach you? _____

What skills, knowledge, or experience could you share with our students?

Are you interested in working:

❑ in the classroom doing a presentation?

❑ with a small group of interested students on a project?

❑ with an individual student on a project?

❑ other? (Please explain.)

Are you available:

❑ during the school day?

❑ directly before or after school?

❑ at other times or through media such as instant messaging? (Please explain.)

Would you be willing to provide weekly, ongoing advice and feedback (in person or via telephone or email) to a student working on a project in your area of interest or expertise?

❑ Yes   ❑ No

Teaching as a Creative Activity

A teacher once asked me where he could buy differentiated activities for his middle school students. He told me he didn't think he was good at coming up with new activities. He didn't trust his creative spirit.

Teaching is a creative activity: working with the curriculum and coming up with new ideas for instruction have kept me in education for over 30 years. The act of differentiating instruction captures the creative spirit. There are no reproducible activities for sale that can meet the needs of the students in your classroom as well as you can. **You know who your students are, what they need, and how to design learning that addresses their needs and capitalizes on their strengths.**

I believe that differentiating instruction can energize your students and invigorate your teaching. It takes energy, flexibility, and the willingness to take risks, but the potential rewards for your students are too good to pass up. Teaching is a creative act. It can't be bought.

Some of you may have picked up this book looking for new teaching ideas. Some may be struggling to meet the needs of learners in increasingly diverse classrooms. Whatever your reason, **each of you cares about your students and wants to increase their chances for becoming successful learners.** Along the way, remember to celebrate small steps. Share your ideas with colleagues; send them by email to a teacher in another building; launch them on your school website for sharing across the district. And I would love to hear the results of your creative work. Let me know how you've been using the strategies and send me samples of differentiation techniques you've developed. At the same time, feel free to give me feedback about this book and tell me what's working for you. You can reach me in care of my publisher:

Free Spirit Publishing Inc.
217 Fifth Avenue North, Suite 200
Minneapolis, MN 55401-1299
help4kids@freespirit.com

I would be pleased if this book becomes a valued resource for you. My hope is that its ideas, suggestions, and strategies have answered some of your questions, responded to your concerns, and nurtured your creative spirit.

Letter to Families

Dear Parent or Guardian,

This year I will be getting to know your son or daughter as a learner and as an individual with special interests and learning needs. I'll be asking you to help me by returning a checklist with your perspectives on your child's interests and learning preferences. My purpose is to increase my students' interest in and excitement about learning and, most importantly, to help them be successful in school.

This school year you will see or hear about the teaching ideas I am using to better meet the needs of all my students. Students will be learning in a variety of ways. Sometimes we'll all be working together; at other times, students will be working in small groups, with a partner, or on their own. For group work, they will sometimes choose who to work with and what project they want to tackle. Other times, I will form groups and assign projects based on what students know, what they need to learn, or how they prefer to learn. All students will be offered challenging learning experiences and all will be actively involved in their learning.

My goal is to provide opportunities for all students to be successful and to enjoy learning. Students love both variety in learning and taking on new challenges. They learn at different paces. And they all have preferences about how they like to learn and how they like to show what they have learned. I will be doing my professional best this year to attend to differences among students, trying to ensure that each student is a successful, confident learner.

Please feel free to call or email me with questions or comments. I would enjoy hearing from you.

Sincerely,

Differentiating Classroom Discussions

An easy first step in differentiation is to increase the challenge and variety of your class discussions. The best way to differentiate discussions is to design questions that stretch your students' thinking and challenge their perspectives and understanding. By paying particular attention to the kinds of questions you ask students, you can stimulate learning with a wide range of abilities and readiness. You can also ensure that all lessons are engaging for students and that all emphasize critical and creative thinking.

Using Classroom Questions to Differentiate Learning

You can use a blank matrix plan (pages 86–87) as a prompt to help develop questions for a particular lesson or unit. The verbs associated with each of Bloom's thinking levels can suggest ways to make your questions more challenging and intriguing. By writing your questions under the appropriate headings, you'll see at a glance whether, for example, a lesson provides sufficient opportunity for students to think at higher levels of challenge.

Think about the students in your class. Avoid directing lower-level questions to more advanced students; keep them more actively engaged with challenging questions. This doesn't mean that academically average or struggling students should always be asked low-level questions. All students can learn to think at higher levels with practice and do so readily when a topic interests them. Just as you develop tiered activities that, at a minimum, ask students to apply their knowledge, use classroom questions that stretch all students beyond simple recall or basic comprehension.

Short Shots

Photocopy the list of question stems on page 156, Short Shots: Questions to Challenge Thinking. Use them to engage your students in creative thinking, analytical work, evaluative work, and problem solving. Keep the list in your lesson plan book or laminate it for use during class discussions and to carry with you during small-group or individual work time. Devise questions to supplement those suggested by your text or curriculum guide, which may be at low levels. Use them to keep your discussions and more informal interactions with students both thought-provoking and lively.

Questions to Stimulate Creative Thinking

School tends to be a place that rewards convergent, one-right-answer kinds of thinking. However, our divergent thinkers, the ones who look for all the possibilities, are sometimes not given the chance to use their particular thinking talents. Furthermore, creativity is not some trait that one either has or doesn't have. Creative thinking skills can be learned and developed through practice. You can help by fashioning questions that call for creative thinking.

Here are some general question stems to bring out creative thinking:

1. Creative production questions

How many different _____ can you list?

What are different ways . . . ?

In what ways might . . . ?

What are all the ways . . . ?

2. Analogy questions

How is _____ like _____?

Why is _____ like _____?

What are all the ways that _____ is like _____?

3. Reorganization questions

What if . . . ?

What do you think would happen if . . . and why?

How/why do you suppose . . . ?

4. Viewpoint/Perspective questions

Would you rather be _____ or _____? Why?

Would you like to be _____? Why or why not?

How would this look from the viewpoint of _____?

If you were _____, what would you do?

As with all the techniques of differentiated instruction, the questions you ask during class discussions need to relate to your curriculum. Creative thinking should be integrated into your instructional plans, not used in isolation or treated as a fun extra activity. Following are examples of creative thinking questions dealing with two specific topics or units: science fiction/fantasy literature and simple machines.

Creative questions for science fiction/ fantasy literature

- What are some different ways that the main character might have solved the major problem(s) presented in the story?

- How is a science fiction (or fantasy) story like a medieval tapestry?

- What would happen if the story had been set in a different time period or different setting? How would that affect the plot or character development?

- How do you think the story would change if the main character were the opposite gender? If the main character were much older or much younger? Why?

- What if a character from another science fiction (or fantasy) book you've read or film you've seen entered this story? How might the story change?

- Would you rather be the antagonist or the protagonist of this story? Why?

Creative questions for simple machines

- What if simple machines did not exist? Think through your morning preparations for school. In what ways would your day start off differently?

- How is force like a blizzard? How is it like a tropical storm?

- How might a pulley or inclined plane make your day at school easier?

- If you were a toy designer, how could a simple machine make a remote control race car work better or be more fun to use? What simple machines might you use in redesigning the race car and its accessories?

Brainstorming

Most teachers use brainstorming from time to time. The rules of brainstorming are based on thinking skills related to creativity: fluency, flexibility, originality, and elaboration. Fluency means coming up with as many ideas as possible. Flexibility means coming up with different kinds of ideas. Originality means coming up with unique, unusual ideas. Elaboration means adding details to an idea or making it new.

Use brainstorming regularly to encourage and nurture creative thinking in your classroom.

Learning Dialogues

Learning dialogues are special kinds of class discussions that can add variety and challenge to your whole-class instruction. Dialogue is a communication process built on trust and respect that promotes a group's ability to think and learn together. Learning dialogues differ from typical classroom discussions because they emphasize the open exchange of ideas rather than "right" answers. They differ from debates because they're collaborative rather than competitive. Dialogues challenge thinking and develop analytical abilities. They also enhance the skills of cooperation and flexibility; encourage respect for others' opinions and perspectives; and stimulate students' desire to pursue new knowledge or understand more deeply. Learning dialogues enable students to "get their voice" in the classroom. They are a natural for differentiated classrooms, since while all students participate, they do so based on their own knowledge, understanding, and perspectives. Dialogue reveals both commonalities and differences in learners, helping you be more responsive to students' needs.

Think about the parts of your course or curriculum that could benefit from this form of in-depth conversation. What topics would lend themselves to lively dialogue? Are there current issues or problems that could provide real-life examples or applications of curriculum topics? Could your students have a dialogue about a historical decision or the ethics of a protagonist in a novel? Once learning dialogues become part of your teaching repertoire, you'll find many uses for them.

Use learning dialogues as a whole-group activity or divide your class into two groups: one to participate in the dialogue and the other to observe and provide feedback. Distribute the Observer's Checklist on page 157 and assign each student in the observer group a partner in the dialogue group. Observers watch the participation of their partners and then fill out the checklist to give to them after the dialogue. For the next dialogue, roles are reversed.

Student Guidelines for Dialogue

Students need to be aware of the conditions necessary for effective learning dialogues. Discuss the following guidelines with students, refer to them as necessary during a dialogue, and use them for your debriefing session after a dialogue.

1. Accept that there is more than one way to look at something and often more than one right answer. Don't make assumptions. Stay open to others' ideas and viewpoints.

2. Listen. The best way to understand something is to listen carefully and thoughtfully.

3. Base your ideas on evidence. Use your personal experience as evidence when appropriate to the topic.

4. Ask for clarification if you don't understand something. ("Tell me more about . . . " "What did you mean when you said . . . ?")

5. Treat each other as equals. Welcome all ideas. Give everyone time and opportunity to participate.

6. Focus on the conversation, not on your position or opinion. Your role is not to win or persuade others—your role is to share your ideas. On some topics, agree to disagree.

7. The sole purpose of a learning dialogue is to share ideas with classmates about a particular topic. It's not necessary to reach agreement or come to the same conclusion. You are trying to deepen your understanding.

Questions to Spark Dialogue

The questions you ask students during learning dialogues are important ways to spark the give-and-take of these interchanges. Here are some guidelines for developing the kinds of questions you need for an authentic dialogue.

F I G U R E   3 0

Questions to Spark Dialogue

Clarification

■ What is meant by _____?

■ What are the big ideas in _____?

■ Give an example of _____.

■ Tell us more about _____.

■ How does _____ relate to _____?

■ How could you say that another way?

■ Summarize what _____ said.

■ What do you think is the main problem/issue in _____?

■ What is the main point of _____?

■ Explain what you think about _____.

■ Why do you think _____ happened?

■ What do you think the author means by _____?

■ What does the term _____ mean?

■ What does the author want you to believe? What evidence can you find for that conclusion?

■ What does the reading say about _____? What do you believe? Why?

Checking Assumptions

■ What assumptions are being made?

■ Is this always true?

■ What are some other perspectives or viewpoints on this?

Providing Reasons and Evidence

■ How do you know?

■ Why do you think that is true?

■ Give reasons. Why?

■ What other information do we need?

■ How could we find out _____?

■ Can you think of an example to illustrate _____?

■ Do you agree? Disagree? Why?

■ Explain.

■ How could we prove or confirm that?

■ What support can you find for that idea?

Examining Viewpoints

■ Why do you believe that?

■ What might be another point of view?

■ How would this be viewed from the perspective of _____?

■ What is an alternative? Another way?

■ How are these ideas alike? Different?

■ What about _____?

■ What feelings or emotions might have caused _____?

■ The author said _____. What do you think?

Investigating Implications and Consequences

■ What might happen if _____?

■ If _____ happened, what would be the result? Support your conclusion.

■ What would be the effects of _____?

■ What conclusions can you make concerning _____?

■ In what way would _____ change if _____ happened?

■ What would be an alternative?

Facilitating Learning Dialogues

Teachers serve as facilitators in learning dialogues. Your role as a facilitator is to keep your students "in dialogue." Here are guidelines for effectively facilitating learning dialogues:

1. Plan about 10 minutes for a typical learning dialogue. Extend the time to 20 minutes for especially rich topics or when students have had some experience with the procedure.

2. Consider: What do you want them to explore in this conversation? Remember

that learning dialogues focus on ideas, values, issues, and perspectives, not on right answers. Decide what specific content students will discuss. To prepare for a dialogue, students need a foundation of knowledge about a topic. Depending on the topic, you might ask them to review class notes, reread pages from a textbook, or check resource material on a subject.

3. Select a good opening question to awaken curiosity, invite thought, and get students engaged in the conversation.

4. Provide time for students to think before they answer. Don't move on too quickly.

5. Restate or rephrase questions if necessary for understanding. Keep the conversation going by asking follow-up questions.

6. Take notes so you can present new questions that spring from the dialogue.

7. Ask students for reasons and evidence to support their ideas.

8. Expect and ask for clear, detailed responses. Encourage elaboration.

9. Expect rigorous thinking. Push, prod, and restate questions to get students there.

10. Expect active listening and engagement. Invite students into the conversation by directing questions toward those who have not participated.

11. Add variety by having everyone respond to a yes/no, agree/disagree question with thumbs up or down. Then ask for clarification or support of their response. ("Why did you agree?")

12. Accept all responses without judgment.

13. If students digress, keep them on the topic with new or restated questions.

14. Help students see relationships between ideas. Weave the conversation together.

15. Encourage discussion of differences of opinion, but discourage argument. A dialogue is not a debate. The goal is to share ideas, not to reach consensus. As necessary, remind students of the guidelines.

16. At appropriate times, ask students to summarize another's ideas in order to pull thoughts together.

17. Correct misinformation by asking clarifying questions.

18. Supply information when necessary to move a dialogue forward, but don't "teach." Keep your comments short and to the point.

Provide Feedback

After a dialogue, conduct a debriefing discussion. Ask students to reflect on how the dialogue went and whether the guidelines were followed. Set goals for improving the process the next time a dialogue is conducted. If your class has been divided into two groups for the dialogue, allow time for observers to share their checklists with participants.

Encourage Self-Reflection

You may wish to ask students to reflect on learning dialogues in writing. Distribute Self-Reflection: Learning Dialogue, page 158.

Follow-Up Projects

Depending on the topic of the learning dialogue, you might wish to follow up by assigning related projects. For example:

1. Newspaper article

2. Video news report

3. Editorial cartoon

4. Caricatures of key figures

5. Storyboard of events

6. Treaties, agreements, contracts

7. Mock trial

8. Debate

9. Letter to the editor

10. Video recorded or written investigative report

11. Testimonial video

12. Reenactment skit

13. Town meeting

14. Point/Counterpoint

Short Shots: Questions to Challenge Thinking

What do you believe and why?

What should be done next and why?

Why do you think that's the answer? Explain.

How can we find out about _____?

Why do you think that about _____?

What would you do about _____ and why?

What are some other ways?

What is the most . . .

   useful and why?

   interesting and why?

   effective and why?

   logical and why?

   creative and why?

What are the possible causes of _____?

What are the possible consequences or effects of _____?

What conclusions could you draw of _____?

How would you _____?

How could you _____?

How would you propose a plan to _____?

How would you formulate a solution to _____?

How would you defend _____?

How would you state the problem?

How would you support your conclusion?

Observer's Checklist

Observer: _____

Participant: _____

Did the participant:

___ appear to be well prepared?

___ present ideas, not opinions?

___ make relevant comments and stay on the subject?

___ use evidence or examples to support ideas?

___ ask for clarification when needed?

___ encourage others to participate?

___ listen carefully to others?

___ speak loudly and clearly?

___ stay engaged in the conversation?

___ talk to other participants, not just the facilitator?

___ stay open to others' ideas?

___ show respect for others?

What was the best point the participant made during the dialogue?

What did the participant do well?

What speaking and listening skills should the participant keep in mind for the next learning dialogue?

Self-Reflection: Learning Dialogue

Name: _____

Date: _____

Topic of Dialogue: _____

What was the most interesting question asked?

What was the most interesting idea you heard from another participant?

Was there anything that puzzled or confused you? Describe it.

How did you contribute to our dialogue today?

What would you do differently next time?

What should we change next time to make our dialogue better?

Content Catalysts, Processes, and Products (CCPP) Toolkit

An alternative method that you may wish to use for designing differentiated activities is the CCPP Toolkit. The toolkit includes lists of content catalysts (CC) processes (P) and products (P), which are combined in a menu-like approach to create differentiated activities. (See Figure 31, page 160.)

Catalysts are ways to introduce your students to content. If students always read from their textbooks or you most frequently present a mini-lecture, you may want to introduce more variety to the mode of learning. Content catalysts are lists of ways to present content to your students and actively engage them in the learning process. Referring to the catalyst list as you construct differentiated activities encourages you to use a variety of ways to engage your students in learning. The process list includes verbs that ask your students to use higher-level thinking. Choosing process verbs from this list directs the level of challenge of the learning activity. The product list represents a variety of Gardner's intelligences. While not a comprehensive list, it will help you "move around" products so that your students can show their learning in many different ways.

To use the toolkit, consider your content and then choose words from each list to construct a learning activity: content catalyst + process verb + product. You can use the lists of catalysts, process verbs, and products as a menu for creating learning activities, choosing a word or two from each list. For example, if you are teaching a unit on personal fitness and health, you may create the following learning activity using the lists:

> After reviewing tobacco company advertisements and identifying their techniques for persuasion, students design an antismoking campaign that appeals to middle schoolers.

Advertisements was chosen from the content catalyst list, *design* from the process list, and *campaign* from the product list. Other examples include:

- After examining wordless picture books (content catalyst), students create (process) a comic strip (product) telling a story without words.

- After examining articles and quotations (content catalysts) related to American Indian experiences during westward expansion, students determine (process) the perspectives of an American Indian tribe and write an editorial (product) reflecting their viewpoints.

- After using computer software (content catalyst) to solve logic problems, students develop (process) an original logic problem and solution (product) involving at least three people, their favorite school activities or subjects, and their favorite coaches or teachers.

The toolkit's lists enable teachers to both quickly and effectively create learning activities that reflect both variety and challenge.

FIGURE 31

The CCPP Toolkit

Directions: Choose one content catalyst, one process, and one product to design differentiated activities.

Content Catalysts

advertisement, commercial
anecdote
application for an iPad or
    smartphone
art activity
article
artifact
artwork
autobiography
biography
case study
chart, graph
comic strip or cartoon
computer software
dance, creative movement, or
    drama performance

demonstration
diagram
display
editorial
editorial cartoon
ethical or moral dilemma
excerpt
excerpt from a speech
exhibit or collection of items
fable, folk tale, myth
field trip (virtual or onsite)
historical fiction
interview
letter to editor
metaphor, analogy

mini-lecture
model or diagram
moral dilemma
movement
movie or video clip
newspaper
novel
open-ended question
panel discussion
picture, photograph,
    illustration
picture book
plan
poetry
PowerPoint presentation

problem situation
profiles of people from
    books or magazines
provocative question
quotations
scenario
simulation (online or in class)
slogan
song or piece of music
speaker
story
survey or research results
time line
website

Processes

adapt
analyze
appraise
assess
calculate
categorize
choose
classify
compare/contrast
compose
construct
convert
create
critique
decide
deduce
demonstrate
design
detect

determine
develop
diagram
differentiate
distinguish
dramatize
employ
estimate
evaluate
examine
experiment
express
forecast
formulate
hypothesize
illustrate
implement
incorporate
infer

initiate
innovate
integrate
interpret
invent
investigate
judge
justify
make
manipulate
model
operate
organize
practice
predict
prioritize
produce
question
rate

record
refine
reflect
reformat
research
respond
review
revise
select
sequence/order
solve
support
synthesize
transform
translate
use
value
verify
write

Products

advertisement or sales pitch
advice column
animated story or presentation
book jacket or film poster
campaign for product or
    candidate
comic strip or graphic novel
costume or set design
critical review

demonstration
diagram or chart
digital music
experiment
fairy tale/folktale/legend
formula
guidebook
investigative report
journal entry

limerick
log or record
magazine or journal article
mask
multimedia presentation
oral presentation
photo essay
pictorial tour
play or skit

personal viewpoint or
    perspective
policy statement
PowerPoint presentation
puppet show
radio talk show
rhyme/riddle/jingle
slogan
virtual fieldtrip

Adapted from original work of Diane Heacox, Sarah J. Noonan, and Gilbert Valdez, 1991.

References and Resources

Anderson, L. & Krathwohl, D. (2000). *A Taxonomy for Learning, Teaching, and Assessing: A Revision of Bloom's Taxonomy of Educational Objectives.* Boston: Allyn & Bacon.

Armstrong, T. (2009). *Multiple Intelligences in the Classroom.* Alexandria, VA: Association for Supervision and Curriculum Development.

Banks, J. (2008). *Teaching Strategies for Ethnic Studies.* Boston: Allyn & Bacon.

Bender, W. (2002). *Differentiating Instruction for Students with Learning Disabilities: Best Teaching Practices for General and Special Educators.* Thousand Oaks, CA: Corwin Press.

Bender, W. & Shores, C. (2007). *Response to Intervention: A Practical Guide for Every Teacher.* Thousand Oaks, CA: Corwin Press.

Bloom, B., editor (1984). *Taxonomy of Educational Objectives: Book 1 Cognitive Domain.* New York: Addison Wesley Longman.

Cash, R. (2011). *Advancing Differentiation: Thinking and Learning for the 21st Century.* Minneapolis: Free Spirit Publishing.

Chapman, C., and Freeman, L. (1996). *Multiple Intelligences Centers and Projects.* Arlington Heights, IL: Skylight Professional Development.

Coil, C. (2011). *Differentiated Activities and Assessments Using the Common Core Standards.* Saline, MI: Pieces of Learning.

Crawford, J. (2011). *Aligning Your Curriculum to the Common Core State Standards.* Thousand Oaks, CA: Corwin Press.

Dacey, L. & Gartland, K. (2009). *Math for All: Differentiating Instruction Grades 6-8.* Sausalito, CA: Math Solutions

Dacey, L. & Lynch, J. (2009). *Math for All: Differentiating Instruction Grades 3-5.* Sausalito, CA: Math Solutions.

Dacey, L. & Salemi, R. (2009). *Math for All: Differentiating Instruction Grades K-2.* Sausalito, CA: Math Solutions.

Dean, C., Hubbell, E., Pitler, H. & Stone, B. (2012). *Classroom Instruction That Works: Research-Based Strategies for Increasing Student Achievement.* Alexandria, VA: Association for Supervision and Curriculum Development.

Dembo, M. (1994). *Applying Educational Psychology in the Classroom.* New York: Longman.

Diller, D. (2003). *Literacy Work Stations: Making Centers Work.* Portland, ME: Stenhouse Publishers.

Diller, D. (2005). *Practice with Purpose: Literacy Work Stations for Grades 3-6.* Portland, ME: Stenhouse Publishers.

Drapeau, P. (2009). *Differentiating with Graphic Organizers: Tools to Foster Critical and Creative Thinking.* Thousand Oaks, CA: Corwin Press.

Dunn, R. & Dunn, K. (1992). *Teaching Elementary Students Through Their Individual Learning Styles: Practical Approaches for Grades 3-6.* Boston: Allyn & Bacon.

Dunn, R. & Dunn, K. (1993). *Teaching Secondary Students Through Their Individual Learning Styles: Practical Approaches for Grades 7-12.* Boston: Allyn & Bacon.

Eberle, B. (2008). *SCAMPER: Creative Games and Activities for Imagination Development* (Combined Edition). Waco, TX: Prufrock.

Fisher, D. & Frey, N. (2007). *Checking for Understanding: Formative Assessment Techniques for Your Classroom.* Alexandria, VA: Association for Supervision and Curriculum Development.

Gardner, H. (2011). *Frames of Mind: The Theory of Multiple Intelligences.* New York: Basic Books.

Gardner, H. (2000). *Intelligence Reframed: Multiple Intelligences for the 21st Century.* New York: Basic Books.

Gardner, H. (2006). *Multiple Intelligences: New Horizons in Theory and Practice.* New York: Basic Books.

Gay, G. (2010). *Culturally Responsive Teaching: Theory, Research, and Practice.* New York: Teachers College Press.

Good, T. & Brophy, J. (2007). *Looking in Classrooms.* Boston: Allyn & Bacon.

Gurian, M. (2010). *Boys and Girls Learn Differently!* San Francisco: Jossey-Bass.

Hayes Jacobs, H. (ed.) (2004). *Getting Results with Curriculum Mapping.* Alexandria, VA: Association for Supervision and Curriculum Development.

Hayes Jacobs, H. (1997). *Mapping the Big Picture: Integrating Curriculum and Assessment K-12.* Alexandria, VA: Association for Supervision and Curriculum Development.

Heacox, D. (2009). *Making Differentiation a Habit: How to Ensure Success in Academically Diverse Classrooms.* Minneapolis: Free Spirit Publishing.

Heacox, D. (1991). *Up from Underachievement.* Minneapolis: Free Spirit Publishing.

Hill, J. & Flynn, K. (2006). *Classroom Instruction That Works with English Language Learners.* Alexandria, VA: Association for Supervision and Curriculum Development.

Karnes, F. & Bean, S. (eds.) (2008). *Methods and Materials for Teaching the Gifted.* Waco, TX: Prufrock.

Karnes, F., Stephens, K., Reis, S., & Renzulli, J. (2005). *Curriculum Compacting: An Easy Start to Differentiating of High-Potential Students.* Waco, TX: Prufrock.

Kendall, J. (2011). *Understanding Common Core State Standards.* Denver, CO: McREL.

Magnar, L. (2000). "Reaching All Children Through Differentiated Assessment: The 2-5-8 Plan." *Gifted Child Today* vol. 23, no. 3.

Marzano, R. (2007). *The Art and Science of Teaching*. Alexandria, VA: Association for Supervision and Curriculum Development.

Marzano, R. (2006). *Classroom Assessment and Grading That Work*. Alexandria, VA: Association for Supervision and Curriculum Development.

Marzano, R. (2000). *Transforming Classroom Grading*. Alexandria, VA: Association for Supervision and Curriculum Development.

Marzano, R., Pickering, D., & McTighe, J. (1993). *Assessing Student Outcomes*. Alexandria, VA: Association for Supervision and Curriculum Development.

Marzano, R., Pickering, D. & Pollock, J. (2000). *Classroom Instruction That Works*. Alexandria, VA: Association for Supervision and Curriculum Development.

McTighe, J., & Wiggins, G. (1998). *Understanding by Design*. Alexandria, VA: Association for Supervision and Curriculum Development.

National Governors Association & Council of Chief State School Officers (2012). Common Core State Standards. Retrieved from www.corestandards.org.

O'Connor, K. (2009). *How to Grade for Learning: K–12*. Boston: Allyn & Bacon.

Reis, S., Renzulli, J. & Burns, D. (1992). *Curriculum Compacting: The Complete Guide for Modifying the Regular Curriculum for High Ability Students*. Mansfield Center, CT: Creative Learning Press.

Renzulli, J. (1997). *The Interest-A-Lyzer*. Mansfield, CT: Creative Learning Press.

Renzulli, J. & Rizza, M. (1997). *The Primary Interest-A-Lyzer*. Mansfield, CT: Creative Learning Press.

Renzulli, J. & Smith, L. (1978). *The Compactor*. Mansfield, CT: Creative Learning Press.

Rogers, K. (1990). *Challenges of Promise*. (Title II Research Report). Edina, MN: Edina Public Schools.

Small, M. (2012). *Good Questions: Great Ways to Differentiate Mathematics Instruction*. New York: Teachers College Press.

Small, M. & Lin, A. (2012). *More Good Questions: Great Ways to Differentiate Secondary Mathematics Instruction*. New York: Teachers College Press.

Smutny, J. (2004). *Differentiating for the Young Child: Teaching Strategies Across the Content Areas, PreK–3*. Thousand Oaks, CA: Corwin Press.

Stiggins, R., Arter, J., Chappuis, J., & Chappuis, S. (2012). *Classroom Assessment for Student Learning: Doing It Right—Using It Well*. Boston: Pearson.

Strickland, C. (2007). *Tools for High-Quality Differentiated Instruction: An ASCD Action Tool*. Alexandria, VA: Association for Supervision and Curriculum Development.

Thomas, E. (2010). *Styles and Strategies for Teaching High School Mathematics: 21 Techniques for Differentiating Instruction and Assessment*. Thousand Oaks, CA: Corwin Press.

Thomas, E. (2010). *Styles and Strategies for Teaching Middle School Mathematics: 21 Techniques for Differentiating Instruction and Assessment*. Thousand Oaks, CA: Corwin Press.

Tomlinson, C. (1999). *The Differentiated Classroom: Responding to the Needs of All Learners*. Alexandria, VA: Association for Supervision and Curriculum Development.

Tomlinson, C. (2003). *Fulfilling the Promise of the Differentiated Classroom: Strategies and Tools for Responsive Teaching*. Alexandria, VA: Association for Supervision and Curriculum Development.

Tomlinson, C. (2001). *How to Differentiate Instruction in Mixed Ability Classrooms*. Alexandria, VA: Association for Supervision and Curriculum Development.

Tomlinson, C. & Imbeau, M. (2010). *Leading and Managing a Differentiated Classroom*. Alexandria, VA: Association for Supervision and Curriculum Development.

Tomlinson, C. & McTighe, J. (2006). *Integrating Differentiated Instruction & Understanding by Design: Connecting Content and Kids*. Alexandria, VA: Association for Supervision and Curriculum Development.

Tomlinson, C. & Sousa, D. (2011). *Differentiation and the Brain: How Neuroscience Supports the Learner-Friendly Classroom*. Bloomington, IN: Solution Tree.

Tomlinson, C. & Strickland, C. (2005). *Differentiation in Practice: A Resource Guide for Differentiating Curriculum, Grades 9–12*. Alexandria, VA: Association for Supervision and Curriculum Development.

VanTassel-Baska, J. & Little, C. (eds.) (2010). *Content-Based Curriculum for High-Ability Learners*. Waco, TX: Prufrock.

Wiggins, G. & McTighe, J. (2005). *Understanding by Design*. Alexandria, VA: Association for Supervision and Curriculum Development.

Winebrenner, S. (2009). *Teaching Kids with Learning Difficulties in the Regular Classroom*. Minneapolis: Free Spirit Publishing.

Winebrenner, S. & Brulles, D. (2012). *Teaching Gifted Kids in Today's Classroom: Strategies and Techniques Every Teacher Can Use*. Minneapolis: Free Spirit Publishing.

Wormeli, R. (2007). *Differentiation: From Planning to Practice Grades 6–12*. Portland, ME: Stenhouse Publishers. Westerville, OH: National Middle School Association.

Wormeli, R. (2006). *Fair Isn't Always Equal: Assessing and Grading in the Differentiated Classroom*. Portland, ME: Stenhouse Publishers. Westerville, OH: National Middle School Association.

Wormeli, R. (2005). *Summarization in Any Subject*. Alexandria, VA: Association for Supervision and Curriculum Development.

Index

About the Author

Dr. Diane Heacox is an associate professor of education at St. Catherine University in St. Paul, Minnesota. She is a consultant and professional development trainer to both public and private schools on a variety of topics related to teaching and learning. She is also the author of *Making Differentiation a Habit,* which earned the Association of Education Publishers Distinguished Achievement Award.

Dr. Heacox has taught at both elementary and secondary school levels and has served as a gifted education teacher and administrator, as well as an instructional specialist in public education. Her books have been translated into Dutch, Hungarian, Korean, and Portuguese.

Dr. Heacox serves on the Board of Directors of the Minnesota Association of Supervision and Curriculum Development and the Minnesota Department of Education Gifted Education Advisory Board. She is the past chair for the Middle Level Network and member of the Education committee for NAGC and the facilitator of the Higher Education Division for ASCD.

Dr. Heacox was recognized by the Minnesota Educators of Gifted and Talented as a Friend of the Gifted for service to gifted education. She is also in the University of St. Thomas Educators Hall of Fame for contributions to the field of education.

Other Great Products from Free Spirit

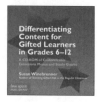